Praise for Accelerate

"This is the kind of foresight that CEOs, CFOs, and CIOs desperately need if their company is going to survive in this new software-centric world.

Anyone that doesn't read this book will be replaced by someone who has."

—Thomas A. Limoncelli, coauthor of *The Practice of Cloud System Administration*

"'Here, do this!' The evidence presented in Accelerate *is a triumph of research, tenacity, and insight, proving not just correlation but a causal link between good technical and management behaviors and business performance. It also exposes the myth of 'maturity models' and offers a realistic, actionable alternative. As an independent consultant working at the intersection of people, technology, process, and organization design this is manna from heaven!*

As chapter 3 concludes: 'You can act your way *to a better culture by implementing these practices in technology organizations' [emphasis mine]. There is no mystical culture magic, just 24 concrete, specific capabilities that will lead not only to better business results, but more importantly to happier, healthier, more motivated people and an organization people want to work at. I will be giving copies of this book to all my clients."*

—Dan North, independent technology and organization consultant

"Whether they recognize it or not, most organizations today are in the business of software development in one way, shape, or form. And most are being dragged down by slow lead times, buggy output, and complicated features that add expense and frustrate users. It doesn't need to be this way. Forsgren, Humble, and Kim shine a compelling light on the what, why, and how of DevOps so you, too, can experience what outstanding looks and feels like."

—Karen Martin, author of *Clarity First* and *The Outstanding Organization*

"Accelerate *does a fantastic job of explaining not only what changes organizations should make to improve their software delivery performance, but also the why, enabling people at all levels to truly understand how to level up their organizations."*

—Ryn Daniels, Infrastructure Operations Engineer at Travis CI and author of *Effective DevOps*

"The 'art' of constructing a building is a well-understood engineering practice nowadays. However, in the software world, we have been looking for patterns and practices that can deliver the same predictable and reliable results whilst minimising waste and producing the increasingly high performance our businesses demand.

Accelerate *provides research-backed, quantifiable, and real-world principles to create world-class, high-performing IT teams enabling amazing business outcomes.*

Backed by the two leading thought leaders (Kim and Humble) in the DevOps community and world-class research from PhD Forsgren, this book is a highly recommended asset!"

—Jonathan Fletcher, Group CTO, Hiscox

"In their book Accelerate, *Nicole Forsgren, Jez Humble, and Gene Kim don't break any new conceptual ground regarding Agile, Lean, and DevOps. Instead, they provide something that might be even more valuable, which is a look inside the methodological rigor of their data collection and analysis approach which led them to their earlier conclusions on the key capabilities that make IT organizations better contributors to the business. This is a book that I will gladly be placing on my bookshelf next to the other great works by the authors."*

—Cameron Haight, VP and CTO, Americas, VMware

"The organizations that thrive in the future will be those that leverage digital technologies to improve their offerings and operations. Accelerate *summarizes the best metrics, practices, and principles to use for improving software delivery and digital product performance, based on years of well-documented research. We strongly recommend this book to anyone involved in a digital transformation for solid guidance about what works, what doesn't work, and what doesn't matter."*

—Tom Poppendieck and Mary Poppendieck, authors of
the *Lean Software Development* series of books

"With this work, the authors have made a significant contribution to the understanding and application of DevOps. They show that when properly understood, DevOps is more than just a fad or a new name for an old concept. Their work illustrates how DevOps can improve the state of the art in organizational design, software development culture, and systems architecture. And beyond merely showing, they advance the DevOps community's qualitative findings with research-based insights that I have heard from no other source."

—Baron Schwartz, Founder and CEO of VividCortex
and coauthor of *High Performance MySQL*

ACCELERATE

THE SCIENCE BEHIND DEVOPS

ACCELERATE

Building and Scaling High Performing Technology Organizations

Nicole Forsgren, PhD
Jez Humble *and* Gene Kim

IT Revolution
Portland, Oregon

25 NW 23rd Pl, Suite 6314
Portland, OR 97210

First Edition

Printed in the United States of America
24 23 22 21 20 19 7 8 9 10

Cover and book design by Devon Smith

Library of Congress Cataloging-in-Publication Data
Names: Forsgren, Nicole, author. | Humble, Jez, author. | Kim, Gene, author.
Title: Accelerate : the science behind DevOps : building and scaling high performing technology organizations / Nicole Forsgren, PhD, Jez Humble and Gene Kim.
Description: First edition. | Portland, Oregon : IT Revolution, [2018] | Includes bibliographical references and index.
Identifiers: LCCN 2018007766 (print) | LCCN 2017061478 (ebook) | ISBN 9781942788355 (ePub) | ISBN 9781942788362 (Kindle) | ISBN 9781942788379 (web pdf) | ISBN 9781942788331 (trade pbk.)
Subjects: LCSH: Agile software development. | Computer software industry--Management. | Information technology--Management. | Operations research.
Classification: LCC QA76.76.D47 (print) | LCC QA76.76.D47 F69 2018 (ebook) | DDC 005.1--dc23
LC record available at https://lccn.loc.gov/2018007766

ISBN: 9781942788331
eBook ISBN: 9781942788355
Kindle ISBN: 9781942788362
Web PDF ISBN: 9781942788379

For information about special discounts for bulk purchases or for information on booking authors for an event, please visit our website at www.ITRevolution.com.

Accelerate

Contents

Figures

Tables

FOREWORD

By Martin Fowler

A few years ago I read a report that said, "We can now assert with confidence that high IT performance correlates with strong business performance, helping to boost productivity, profitability, and market share." When I read something like that, my usual response is to toss it with great force into the rubbish bin, because that's usually a tell for some bogus bullshit masquerading as science. I hesitated this time, however, for this was the "2014 State of DevOps Report." One of its authors was Jez Humble, a colleague and friend who I knew was equally allergic to this kind of twaddle. (Although I have to confess that another reason for not tossing it was that I was reading it on my iPad.)

So, instead I emailed Jez to find out what lay behind this statement. A few weeks later I was on a call with him and Nicole Forsgren, who patiently walked me though the reasoning. While I'm no expert on the methods they used, she said enough to convince me there was some real analysis going on here, far more than I usually see, even in academic papers. I followed the subsequent State of DevOps reports with interest, but also with growing frustration. The reports gave the results of their work but never contained the explanation that Nicole walked through with me on the phone. This greatly undermined their credibility, as there was little evidence that these reports were based on more than speculation. Finally, those of us that had seen behind the curtains convinced Nicole, Jez, and Gene to reveal their methods by writing this book. For me, it's been a long wait, but I'm glad I now have something that I can genuinely recommend as a way to look at IT delivery effectiveness—one that's based on more than a few analysts' scattered experiences.

The picture they paint is compelling. They describe how effective IT delivery organizations take about an hour to get code from "committed to mainline" to "running in production," a journey lesser organizations take months to do. They, thus, update their software many times a day instead of once every few months, increasing their ability to use software to explore the market, respond to events, and release features faster than their competition. This huge increase in responsiveness does not come at a cost in stability, since these organizations find their updates cause failures at a fraction of the rate of their less-performing peers, and these failures are usually fixed within the hour. Their evidence refutes the bimodal IT notion that you have to choose between speed and stability—instead, speed depends on stability, so good IT practices give you both.

So, as you may expect, I'm delighted that they've put this book into production, and I will be recommending it willy-nilly over the next few years. (I've already been using many bits from its drafts in my talks.) However, I do want to put in a few notes of caution. They do a good job of explaining why their approach to surveys makes them a good basis for their data. However, they are still surveys that capture subjective perceptions, and I wonder how their population sample reflects the general IT world. I'll have more confidence in their results when other teams, using different approaches, are able to confirm their reasoning. The book already has some of this, as the work done by Google on team cultures provides further evidence to support their judgment on how important a Westrum-generative organizational culture is for effective software teams. Such further work would also make me less concerned that their conclusions confirm much of my advocacy—confirmation bias is a strong force (although I mostly notice it in others ;-)). We should also remember that their book focuses on IT delivery, that is, the journey from commit to production, not the entire software development process.

But these quibbles, while present, shouldn't distract us from the main thrust of this book. These surveys, and the careful analysis done on them, provide some of the best justification around for practices that can significantly improve most IT organizations. Anyone running an IT group should take a good hard look at these techniques and work to use them to improve their practice. Anyone working with an IT group, either internally or from an IT delivery company like ours, should look for these practices in place and a steady program of continuous improvement to go with them. Forsgren, Humble, and Kim have laid out a picture of what effective IT looks like in 2017, and IT practitioners should be using this as a map to join the high performers.

Martin Fowler
Chief Scientist, ThoughtWorks

FOREWORD

By Courtney Kissler

My journey started in the summer of 2011. I was working at Nordstrom and we had made a strategic decision to focus on digital as the growth engine. Up until that point, our IT organization was optimized for cost; I shared in my DevOps Enterprise Summit 2014 presentation that one of my "aha" moments was the shift to optimizing for speed. I made a lot of mistakes along the way and wish I had access to the information in this book back then. Common traps were stepped in—like trying a top-down mandate to adopt Agile, thinking it was one size fits all, not focusing on measurement (or the right things to measure), leadership behavior not changing, and treating the transformation like a program instead of creating a learning organization (never done).

Throughout the journey, the focus was moving to outcome-based team structures, knowing our cycle time (by understanding our value stream map), limiting the blast radius (starting with one to two teams vs. boiling the ocean), using data to drive actions and decisions, acknowledging that work is work (don't have a backlog of features and a backlog of technical debt and a backlog of operational work; instead, have a single backlog because NFRs are features and reducing technical debt improves stability of the product). None of this happened overnight, and it took a lot of experimentation and adjusting along the way.

What I know to be true based on my experience is that adopting the guidance in this book *will* make your organization higher performing. It works for all types of software delivery and is methodology agnostic. I have personally experienced it and have multiple examples of applying these practices within mainframe environments, traditional packaged software application delivery teams, and product teams. It can work across the board. It takes discipline, persistence, transformational leadership, and a focus on people. After all, people are an organization's #1 asset, but so often that is not how organizations operate. Even though the journey will not be easy, I can say that it is definitely worth it, and not only will you see better results, your team will be happier. As an example, when we started measuring eNPS, the teams practicing these techniques had the highest scores throughout our technology organization.

Another thing I learned along the way is how critical it is to have senior leadership support. And support in actions, not words. Senior leaders need to demonstrate their commitment to creating a learning organization. I will share the behaviors I try to model with my teams. I believe passionately in honoring and extracting reality. If I am a senior leader and my team doesn't feel comfortable sharing risks, then I will never truly know reality. And, if I'm not genuinely curious and only show up when there's a failure, then I am failing as a senior leader. It's important to build trust and to demonstrate that failure leads to inquiry (see the Westrum model in this book).

You will encounter skeptics along the way. I heard things like "DevOps is the new Agile," "Lean doesn't apply to software delivery," "Of course this worked for the mobile app team. They are a unicorn." When I encountered the skeptics, I attempted to use external examples to influence the discussion. I leveraged mentors along the way—without them, it would have been challenging to stay focused. Having the information in this book would have been extremely helpful and I strongly encourage you to use it within your organization. I have spent most of my career in retail; in that industry, it has become more and more critical to evolve, and shipping software is now part of the DNA of every organization. Don't ignore the science outlined in this book. It will help you accelerate your transformation to a high-performing technology organization.

Courtney Kissler
VP Digital Platform Engineering, Nike

QUICK REFERENCE: CAPABILITIES TO DRIVE IMPROVEMENT

Our research has uncovered 24 key capabilities that drive improvements in software delivery performance. This reference will point you to them in the book. A detailed guide is found in Appendix A. They are presented in no particular order.

The capabilities are classified into five categories:

- Continuous delivery
- Architecture
- Product and process
- Lean management and monitoring
- Cultural

CONTINUOUS DELIVERY CAPABILITIES

1. Version control: Chapter 4
2. Deployment automation: Chapter 4
3. Continuous integration: Chapter 4
4. Trunk-based development: Chapter 4
5. Test automation: Chapter 4
6. Test data management: Chapter 4
7. Shift left on security: Chapter 6
8. Continuous delivery (CD): Chapter 4

ARCHITECTURE CAPABILITIES

9. Loosely coupled architecture: Chapter 5
10. Empowered teams: Chapter 5

PRODUCT AND PROCESS CAPABILITIES

11. Customer feedback: Chapter 8
12. Value stream: Chapter 8
13. Working in small batches: Chapter 8
14. Team experimentation: Chapter 8

LEAN MANAGEMENT AND MONITORING CAPABILITIES

15. Change approval processes: Chapter 7
16. Monitoring: Chapter 7
17. Proactive notification: Chapter 13
18. WIP limits: Chapter 7
19. Visualizing work: Chapter 7

CULTURAL CAPABILITIES

20. Westrum organizational culture: Chapter 3
21. Supporting learning: Chapter 10
22. Collaboration among teams: Chapters 3 and 5
23. Job satisfaction: Chapter 10
24. Transformational leadership: Chapter 11

PREFACE

Beginning in late 2013, we embarked on a four-year research journey to investigate what capabilities and practices are important to accelerate the development and delivery of software and, in turn, value to companies. These results are seen in their profitability, productivity, and market share. We see similarly strong effects in noncommercial outcomes of effectiveness, efficiency, and customer satisfaction.

This research fills a need that isn't currently served in the market. By using rigorous research methods traditionally only found in academia, and making it accessible to industry, our goal is to advance the state of software development and delivery. By helping the industry identify and understand the capabilities that actually drive performance improvements in a statistically meaningful way—more than just anecdote, and beyond the experiences of one or a few teams—we can help the industry improve.

To conduct the research found in this book (in addition to research we still actively conduct), we use cross-sectional studies. The same methods are used in healthcare research (e.g., to investigate the relationship between beer and obesity, Bobak et al. 2003), workplace research (e.g., to study the relationship between the work environment and cardiovascular disease, Johnson and Hall 1988), and memory research (e.g., to investigate differences in development and decline in memory, Alloway and Alloway 2013). As we want to truly investigate the industry and understand what drives improvement in software and organizational performance in a meaningful way, we use rigorous academic research design methods and publish much of our work in academic peer-reviewed journals. For more information about the methods used in our research, check out Part II: The Research.

THE RESEARCH

Our research collected over 23,000 survey responses from around the world. We heard from over 2,000 unique organizations, from small startups of under five employees to large enterprises with over 10,000 employees. We collected data from startups and cutting-edge internet companies as well as highly regulated industries, such as finance, healthcare, and government. Our data and analysis includes software developed on brand new "greenfield" platforms as well as legacy code maintenance and development.

The findings in this book will apply whether you're using a traditional "waterfall" methodology (also known as gated, structured, or plan-driven) and just beginning your technology transformation, or whether you have been implementing Agile and DevOps practices for years. This is true because software delivery is an exercise in continuous improvement, and our research shows that year over year the best keep getting better, and those who fail to improve fall further and further behind.

> ***Improvement Is Possible for Everyone***
>
> Our quest to understand how to measure and improve software delivery was full of insights and surprises. The moral of the story, borne out in the data, is this: improvements in software delivery are possible for every team and in every company, as long as leadership provides consistent support—

including time, actions, and resources—demonstrating a true commitment to improvement, and as long as team members commit themselves to the work.

Our goal in writing this book is to share what we have learned so that we can help organizations excel, grow happier teams who deliver better software faster, and help individuals and organizations thrive. The rest of this preface briefly describes the research, how it began, and how it was conducted. More detail about the science behind the study can be found in Part II of this book.

THE JOURNEY AND THE DATA

We are often asked about the genesis story of this research. It is based on a compelling curiosity for what makes high-performing technology organizations great, and how software makes organizations better. Each author spent time on parallel paths working to understand superior technical performance before joining forces in late 2013:

- **Nicole Forsgren** has a PhD in Management Information Systems. Prior to 2013, she spent several years researching the factors that make technology impactful in organizations, particularly among the professionals that make software and support infrastructure. She has authored dozens of peer-reviewed articles on the subject. Before her PhD, she was a software and hardware engineer and a sysadmin.
- **Jez Humble** is the coauthor of *Continuous Delivery*, *Lean Enterprise*, and *The DevOps Handbook*. His first job after college was working at a startup in London in 2000, and

then from 2005–2015 he spent a decade at ThoughtWorks delivering software products and consulting as an infrastructure specialist, developer, and product manager.

- **Gene Kim** has been studying high-performing technology organizations since 1999. He was the founder and CTO of Tripwire for thirteen years and is the coauthor of many books, including *The Phoenix Project* and *The Visible Ops Handbook*.

In late 2013, Nicole, Jez, and Gene started working together with the team at Puppet in preparation for the *2014 State of DevOps Report*.[1] By combining practical expertise and academic rigor, the team was able to generate something unique in the industry: a report containing insights into how to help technology deliver value to employees, organizations, and customers in predictive ways. Over the next four reports, Nicole, Jez, and Gene continued collaborating with the Puppet team to iterate on research design and continuously improve the industry's understanding of what contributes to great software delivery, what enables great technical teams, and how companies can become high-performing organizations and win in the market by leveraging technology. This book covers four years of research findings, starting with that report (2014 through 2017).

[1] It is important to note that the *State of DevOps Report* got its start prior to 2014. In 2012, the team at Puppet Inc. invited Gene to participate in the second iteration of a study it was developing to better understand a little known phenomenon called DevOps, how it was being adopted, and the performance advantages organizations were seeing. Puppet had been a big proponent and driver of the movement as the idea of "DevOps" began to take shape following the first DevOpsDays, discussions on Twitter, and a seminal talk by John Allspaw and Paul Hammond. Gene then invited Jez to join the study, and together they collected and analyzed 4,000 survey responses from around the world, making it the largest survey of its kind.

To collect the data, each year we emailed invitations to our mailing lists and leveraged social media, including Twitter, LinkedIn, and Facebook. Our invitations targeted professionals working in technology, especially those familiar with software development and delivery paradigms and DevOps. We encouraged our readers to invite friends and peers who might also work in software development and delivery to help us broaden our reach. This is called snowball sampling, and we talk about why this was an appropriate data collection method for this research project in Chapter 15, "The Data for the Project."

The data for our project came from surveys. We used surveys because they are the best way to collect a large amount of data from thousands of organizations in a short amount of time. For a detailed discussion of why good research can be conducted from surveys, as well as the steps we took to ensure the data we collected was trustworthy and accurate, see Part II which covers the science and research behind the book.

Here is a brief outline of the research and how it evolved over the years.

2014: LAYING THE FOUNDATION. DELIVERY PERFORMANCE AND ORGANIZATIONAL PERFORMANCE

Our research goals for the first year were to lay a foundation for understanding software development and delivery in organizations. Some key research questions were:

- What does it mean to deliver software, and can it be measured?
- Does software delivery impact organizations?

- Does culture matter, and how do we measure it?
- What technical practices appear to be important?

We were pleasantly surprised by many of the results in the first year. We discovered that software development and delivery can be measured in a statistically meaningful way, and that high performers do it in consistently good ways that are significantly better than many other companies. We also found that throughput and stability move together, and that an organization's ability to make software positively impacts profitability, productivity, and market share. We saw that culture and technical practices matter, and found how to measure them. This is covered in Part I of this book.

The team also revised the way most of the data had been measured in the past, moving from simple yes/no questions to Likert-type questions (in which respondents choose from a range of options from "Strongly Disagree" to "Strongly Agree"). This simple change in survey questions let the team collect more nuanced data—shades of gray instead of black and white. This allowed for more detailed analysis. For a discussion of the authors' choice to use surveys for this research project and why you can trust their survey-based data, see Chapter 14, "Why Use a Survey."

2015: EXTENDING THE WORK AND DEEPENING THE ANALYSIS

Much like technology transformations and business growth, conducting research is all about iteration, incremental improvements, and revalidation of important results. Armed with our findings from the first year, our goals in year two were to revalidate and confirm some key findings (e.g., software delivery can be defined and measured in a statistically meaningful way, software delivery impacts organizational performance) while also extending the model.

These were some of the research questions:

- Can we revalidate that software delivery impacts organizational performance?
- Do technical practices and automation impact software delivery?
- Do lean management practices impact software delivery?
- Do technical practices and Lean management practices impact aspects of work that affect our workforce—such as anxiety associated with code deployments and burnout?

Once again, we got some great confirmations and some surprises. Our hypotheses were supported, confirming and extending the work we had done the previous year. These results can be found in Part I.

2016: EXPANDING OUR LOOK INTO TECHNICAL PRACTICES AND EXPLORING THE FUZZY FRONT END

In year three, we again built on the core foundation of our model and extended it to explore the significance of additional technical practices (such as security, trunk-based development, and test data management). Inspired by conversations with colleagues working in product management, we also extended our investigation further upstream, to see if we could measure the impact of the current move away from traditional project management practices to applying Lean principles in product management. We extended our investigation to include quality measures such as defects, rework, and security remediation. Finally, we included additional questions to help us understand how technical practices influence human capital: employee Net Promoter Score (eNPS) and work identity—a factor that is likely to decrease burnout.

These were our research questions:

- Does the integration of security into software development and delivery help the process or slow it down?
- Does trunk-based development contribute to better software delivery?
- Is a Lean approach to product management an important aspect of software development and delivery?
- Do good technical practices contribute to strong company loyalty?

2017: INCLUDING ARCHITECTURE, EXPLORING THE ROLE OF LEADERS, AND MEASURING SUCCESS IN NOT-FOR-PROFIT ORGANIZATIONS

Year four of the research saw us moving into questions about how systems are architected and the impact architecture has on teams' and organizations' ability to deliver software and value. We also extended our research to include measures of value that extended beyond profitability, productivity, and market share, allowing the analysis to speak to a not-for-profit audience. The research this year also explored the role of leaders to measure the impact of transformational leadership in organizations.

Our driving research questions in year four were:

- What architectural practices drive improvements in software delivery performance?
- How does transformational leadership impact software delivery?
- Does software delivery impact not-for-profit outcomes?

CONCLUSION

We hope that as you read this book you discover, as a technologist and technology leader, the essential components to making your organization better—starting with software delivery. It is through improving our ability to deliver software that organizations can deliver features faster, pivot when needed, respond to compliance and security changes, and take advantage of fast feedback to attract new customers and delight existing ones.

In the chapters that follow, we identify the key capabilities that drive the software delivery performance (and define what software delivery performance is) and briefly touch on the key points in each. Part I of the book presents our findings, Part II discusses the science and research behind our results, and finally, Part III presents a case study of what is possible when organizations adopt and implement these capabilities in order to drive performance.

PART ONE
WHAT WE FOUND

Armed with robust data-gathering and statistical analysis techniques (discussed in detail in Part II), we have been able to discover significant and sometimes surprising results over the past several years working on the State of DevOps Report. We've been able to measure and quantify software delivery performance, its impact on organizational performance, and the various capabilities that contribute to these outcomes.

These capabilities fall into various categories—such as technical, process, and cultural. We've measured the impact of technical practices on culture, and the effect of culture on delivery and organizational performance. For capabilities as disparate as architecture and product management, we've looked at their contribution to these and other important sustainability outcomes such as burnout and deployment pain.

In this part of the book we present our results.

CHAPTER 1

ACCELERATE

"Business as usual" is no longer enough to remain competitive. Organizations in all industries, from finance and banking to retail, telecommunications, and even government, are turning away from delivering new products and services using big projects with long lead times. Instead, they are using small teams that work in short cycles and measure feedback from users to build products and services that delight their customers and rapidly deliver value to their organizations. These high performers are working incessantly to get better at what they do, letting no obstacles stand in their path, even in the face of high levels of risk and uncertainty about how they may achieve their goals.

To remain competitive and excel in the market, organizations must accelerate:

- delivery of goods and services to delight their customers;
- engagement with the market to detect and understand customer demand;
- anticipation of compliance and regulatory changes that impact their systems; and
- response to potential risks such as security threats or changes in the economy.

At the heart of this acceleration is software. This is true of organizations in any industry vertical. Banks no longer deliver value by holding gold bars in vaults but by trading faster and more securely, and by discovering new channels and products to engage customers. Retailers win and retain customers by offering them superior selection and service, with service coming in the form of a fast check-out experience, recommended goods at check-out, or a seamless online/offline shopping experience—all of which are enabled by technology. Government organizations cite the ability to harness technology as the key to serving the public more effectively and efficiently while being parsimonious with taxpayer dollars.

Software and technology are key differentiators for organizations to deliver value to customers and stakeholders. We've found it in our own research outlined in this book—and others have found it, too. For example, a recent study by James Bessen of Boston University found that the strategic use of technology explains revenue and productivity gains more than mergers and acquisitions (M&A) and entrepreneurship (2017). Andrew McAfee and Erik Brynjolfsson have also found a link between technology and profitability (2008).

Software is transforming and accelerating organizations of all kinds. The practices and capabilities we talk about in this book have emerged from what is now known as the DevOps movement, and they are transforming industries everywhere. DevOps emerged from a small number of organizations facing a wicked problem: how to build secure, resilient, rapidly evolving distributed systems at scale. In order to remain competitive, organizations must learn how to solve these problems. We see that large enterprises with long histories and decades-old technologies also gain significant benefits, such as accelerated delivery and lower costs, through adopting the capabilities we outline in this book.

Although many organizations have achieved great success with their technology transformations (notable examples include web-scale tech giants such as Netflix, Amazon, Google, and Facebook, as well as more traditional large organizations including Capital One, Target, and the US Federal Government's Technology Transformation Service and US Digital Service), there is still a lot of work to be done—both in the broader industry and within individual organizations. A recent Forrester (Stroud et al. 2017) report found that 31% of the industry is not using practices and principles that are widely considered to be necessary for accelerating technology transformations, such as continuous integration and continuous delivery, Lean practices, and a collaborative culture (i.e., capabilities championed by the DevOps movement). However, we also know that technology and software transformations are imperative in organizations today. A recent Gartner study found that 47% of CEOs face pressure from their board to digitally transform (Panetta 2017).

Within organizations, technology transformation journeys are at different stages, and reports suggest there is more work to be done than many of us currently believe. Another Forrester report states that DevOps is accelerating technology, but that organizations often overestimate their progress (Klavens et al. 2017). Furthermore, the report points out that executives are especially prone to overestimating their progress when compared to those who are actually doing the work.

These findings about the disconnect between executive and practitioner estimates of DevOps maturity highlight two considerations that are often missed by leaders. First, if we assume the estimates of DevOps maturity or capabilities from practitioners are more accurate—because they are closer to the work—the potential for value delivery and growth within organizations is much greater than executives currently realize. Second, the disconnect makes clear the need to measure DevOps capabilities accurately and to communicate these measurement results to leaders, who can use them to make decisions and inform strategy about their organization's technology posture.

FOCUS ON CAPABILITIES, NOT MATURITY

Technology leaders need to deliver software quickly and reliably to win in the market. For many companies, this requires significant changes to the way we deliver software. The key to successful change is measuring and understanding the right things with a focus on capabilities—not on maturity.

While maturity models are very popular in the industry, we cannot stress enough that maturity models are not the appropriate tool to use or mindset to have. Instead, shifting to a capabilities model of measurement is essential for organizations wanting to accelerate software delivery. This is due to four factors.

First, maturity models focus on helping an organization "arrive" at a mature state and then declare themselves done with their journey, whereas technology transformations should follow a continuous improvement paradigm. Alternatively, capability models focus on helping an organization continually improve and progress, realizing that the technological and business landscape is ever-changing. The most innovative companies and highest-performing organizations are always striving to be better and never consider themselves "mature" or "done" with their improvement or transformation journey—and we see this in our research.

Second, maturity models are quite often a "lock-step" or linear formula, prescribing a similar set of technologies, tooling, or capabilities for every set of teams and organizations to progress through. Maturity models assume that "Level 1" and "Level 2" look the same across all teams and organizations, but those of us who work in technology know this is not the case. In contrast, capability models are multidimensional and dynamic, allowing different parts of the organization to take a customized approach to improvement, and focus on capabilities that will give them the most benefit based on their current context and their short- and long-term goals. Teams have their own context, their own systems, their own goals, and their own constraints, and what we should focus on next to accelerate our transformation depends on those things.

Third, capability models focus on key outcomes and how the capabilities, or levers, drive improvement in those outcomes—that is, they are outcome based. This provides technical leadership with clear direction and strategy on high-level goals (with a focus on capabilities to improve key outcomes). It also enables team leaders and individual contributors to set improvement goals related to the capabilities their team is focusing on for the current time period. Most maturity models simply measure the technical proficiency or tooling install base in an organization without tying it to outcomes. These end up being vanity metrics: while they can be relatively easy to measure, they don't tell us anything about the impact they have on the business.

Fourth, maturity models define a static level of technological, process, and organizational abilities to achieve. They do not take into account the ever-changing nature of the technology and business landscape. Our own research and data have confirmed that the industry is changing: what is good enough and even "high-performing" today is no longer good enough in the next year. In contrast, capability models allow for dynamically changing environments and allow teams and organizations to focus on developing the skills and capabilities needed to remain competitive.

By focusing on a capabilities paradigm, organizations can continuously drive improvement. And by focusing on the *right* capabilities, organizations can drive improvements in their outcomes, allowing them to develop and deliver software with improved speed and stability. In fact, we see that the highest performers do exactly this, continually reaching for gains year over year and never settling for yesterday's accomplishments.

EVIDENCE-BASED TRANSFORMATIONS FOCUS ON KEY CAPABILITIES

Within both capability and maturity model frameworks, there are disagreements about *which* capabilities to focus on. Product vendors often favor capabilities that align with their product offerings. Consultants favor capabilities that align with their background, their offering, and their homegrown assessment tool. We have seen organizations try to design their own assessment models, choose solutions that align with the skill sets of internal champions, or succumb to analysis paralysis because of the sheer number of areas that need improvement in their organization.

A more guided, evidence-based solution is needed, and the approach discussed in this book describes such a solution.

Our research has yielded insights into what enables both software delivery performance and organizational performance as seen in profitability, productivity, and market share. In fact, our research shows that none of the following often-cited factors predicted performance:

- age and technology used for the application (for example, mainframe "systems of record" vs. greenfield "systems of engagement")

- whether operations teams or development teams performed deployments
- whether a change approval board (CAB) is implemented

The things that *do* make a difference in the success of software delivery and organizational performance are those that the highest performers and most innovative companies use to get ahead. Our research has identified 24 key capabilities that drive improvement in software delivery performance and, in turn, organizational performance. These capabilities are easy to define, measure, and improve.[1] This book will get you started on defining and measuring these capabilities. We will also point you to some fantastic resources for improving them, so you can accelerate your own technology transformation journey.

THE VALUE OF ADOPTING DEVOPS

You may be asking yourself: How do we know that these capabilities are drivers of technology and organizational performance, and why can we say it with such confidence?

The findings from our research program show clearly that the value of adopting DevOps is even larger than we had initially thought, and the gap between high and low performers continues to grow.

We discuss how we measure software delivery performance and how our cohort performs in detail in the following chapter. To summarize, in 2017 we found that, when compared to low performers, the high performers have:

[1] These 24 capabilities are listed, along with a pointer to the chapter that discusses them, in Appendix A.

- 46 times more frequent code deployments
- 440 times faster lead time from commit to deploy
- 170 times faster mean time to recover from downtime
- 5 times lower change failure rate (1/5 as likely for a change to fail)

When compared to the 2016 results, the gap between high performers and low performers narrowed for tempo (deployment frequency and change lead time) and widened for stability (mean time to recover and change failure rate). We speculate that this is due to low-performing teams working to increase tempo but not investing enough in building quality into the process. The result is larger deployment failures that take more time to restore service. High performers understand that they don't have to trade speed for stability or vice versa, because by building quality in they get both.

You may be wondering: How do high-performing teams achieve such amazing software delivery performance? They do this by turning the right levers—that is, by improving the right capabilities.

Over our four-year research program we have been able to identify the capabilities that drive performance in software delivery and impact organizational performance, and we have found that they work for all types of organizations. Our research investigated organizations of all sizes, in all industries, using legacy and greenfield technology stacks around the world—so the findings in this book will apply to the teams in your organization too.

CHAPTER 2

MEASURING PERFORMANCE

There are many frameworks and methodologies that aim to improve the way we build software products and services. We wanted to discover what works and what doesn't in a scientific way, starting with a definition of what "good" means in this context. This chapter presents the framework and methods we used to work towards this goal, and in particular the key outcome measures applied throughout the rest of this book.

By the end of this chapter, we hope you'll know enough about our approach to feel confident in the results we present in the rest of the book.

Measuring performance in the domain of software is hard—in part because, unlike manufacturing, the inventory is invisible. Furthermore, the way we break down work is relatively arbitrary, and the design and delivery activities—particularly in the Agile software development paradigm—happen simultaneously. Indeed, it's expected that we will change and evolve our design based on what we learn by trying to implement it. So our first step must be to define a valid, reliable measure of software delivery performance.

THE FLAWS IN PREVIOUS ATTEMPTS TO MEASURE PERFORMANCE

There have been many attempts to measure the performance of software teams. Most of these measurements focus on productivity. In general, they suffer from two drawbacks. First, they focus on *outputs* rather than *outcomes*. Second, they focus on individual or local measures rather than team or global ones. Let's take three examples: lines of code, velocity, and utilization.

Measuring productivity in terms of lines of code has a long history in software. Some companies even required developers to record the lines of code committed per week.[1] However, in reality we would prefer a 10-line solution to a 1,000-line solution to a problem. Rewarding developers for writing lines of code leads to bloated software that incurs higher maintenance costs and higher cost of change. Ideally, we should reward developers for solving business problems with the minimum amount of code—and it's even better if we can solve a problem without writing code at all or by deleting code (perhaps by a business process change). However, minimizing lines of code isn't an ideal measure either. At the extreme, this too has its drawbacks: accomplishing a task in a single line of code that no one else can understand is less desirable than writing a few lines of code that are easily understood and maintained.

With the advent of Agile software development came a new way to measure productivity: velocity. In many schools of Agile, problems are broken down into stories. Stories are then estimated by developers and assigned a number of "points" representing the relative effort expected to complete them. At the end of an

[1] There's a good story about how the Apple Lisa team's management discovered that lines of code were meaningless as a productivity metric: http://www.folklore.org/StoryView.py?story=Negative_2000_Lines_Of_Code.txt.

iteration, the total number of points signed off by the customer is recorded—this is the team's velocity. Velocity is designed to be used as a *capacity planning tool*; for example, it can be used to extrapolate how long it will take the team to complete all the work that has been planned and estimated. However, some managers have also used it as a way to measure team productivity, or even to compare teams.

Using velocity as a productivity metric has several flaws. First, velocity is a relative and team-dependent measure, not an absolute one. Teams usually have significantly different contexts which render their velocities incommensurable. Second, when velocity is used as a productivity measure, teams inevitably work to game their velocity. They inflate their estimates and focus on completing as many stories as possible at the expense of collaboration with other teams (which might decrease their velocity and increase the other team's velocity, making them look bad). Not only does this destroy the utility of velocity for its intended purpose, it also inhibits collaboration between teams.

Finally, many organizations measure utilization as a proxy for productivity. The problem with this method is that high utilization is only good up to a point. Once utilization gets above a certain level, there is no spare capacity (or "slack") to absorb unplanned work, changes to the plan, or improvement work. This results in longer lead times to complete work. Queue theory in math tells us that as utilization approaches 100%, lead times approach infinity—in other words, once you get to very high levels of utilization, it takes teams exponentially longer to get anything done. Since lead time—a measure of how fast work can be completed—is a productivity metric that doesn't suffer from the drawbacks of the other metrics we've seen, it's essential that we manage utilization to balance it against lead time in an economically optimal way.

MEASURING SOFTWARE DELIVERY PERFORMANCE

A successful measure of performance should have two key characteristics. First, it should focus on a global outcome to ensure teams aren't pitted against each other. The classic example is rewarding developers for throughput and operations for stability: this is a key contributor to the "wall of confusion" in which development throws poor quality code over the wall to operations, and operations puts in place painful change management processes as a way to inhibit change. Second, our measure should focus on outcomes not output: it shouldn't reward people for putting in large amounts of busywork that doesn't actually help achieve organizational goals.

In our search for measures of delivery performance that meet these criteria, we settled on four: delivery lead time, deployment frequency, time to restore service, and change fail rate. In this section, we'll discuss why we picked these particular measures.

The elevation of lead time as a metric is a key element of Lean theory. Lead time is the time it takes to go from a customer making a request to the request being satisfied. However, in the context of product development, where we aim to satisfy multiple customers in ways they may not anticipate, there are two parts to lead time: the time it takes to design and validate a product or feature, and the time to deliver the feature to customers. In the design part of the lead time, it's often unclear when to start the clock, and often there is high variability. For this reason, Reinertsen calls this part of the lead time the "fuzzy front end" (Reinertsen 2009). However, the *delivery* part of the lead time—the time it takes for work to be implemented, tested, and delivered—is easier to measure and has a lower variability. Table 2.1 (Kim et al. 2016) shows the distinction between these two domains.

Table 2.1 Design vs. Delivery

Product Design and Development	Product Delivery (Build, Testing, Deployment)
Create new products and services that solve customer problems using hypothesis-driven delivery, modern UX, design thinking.	Enable fast flow from development to production and reliable releases by standardizing work, and reducing variability and batch sizes.
Feature design and implementation may require work that has never been performed before.	Integration, test, and deployment must be performed continuously as quickly as possible.
Estimates are highly uncertain.	Cycle times should be well-known and predictable.
Outcomes are highly variable.	Outcomes should have low variability.

Shorter product delivery lead times are better since they enable faster feedback on what we are building and allow us to course correct more rapidly. Short lead times are also important when there is a defect or outage and we need to deliver a fix rapidly and with high confidence. We measured product delivery lead time as the time it takes to go from code committed to code successfully running in production, and asked survey respondents to choose from one of the following options:

- less than one hour
- less than one day
- between one day and one week
- between one week and one month
- between one month and six months
- more than six months

The second metric to consider is batch size. Reducing batch size is another central element of the Lean paradigm—indeed, it was one of the keys to the success of the Toyota production system. Reducing batch sizes reduces cycle times and variability in flow, accelerates feedback, reduces risk and overhead, improves efficiency, increases motivation and urgency, and reduces costs and schedule growth (Reinertsen 2009, Chapter 5). However, in software, batch size is hard to measure and communicate across contexts as there is no visible inventory. Therefore, we settled on deployment frequency as a proxy for batch size since it is easy to measure and typically has low variability.[2] By "deployment" we mean a software deployment to production or to an app store. A release (the changes that get deployed) will typically consist of multiple version control commits, unless the organization has achieved a single-piece flow where each commit can be released to production (a practice known as continuous deployment). We asked survey respondents how often their organization deploys code for the primary service or application they work on, offering the following options:

- on demand (multiple deploys per day)
- between once per hour and once per day
- between once per day and once per week
- between once per week and once per month
- between once per month and once every six months
- fewer than once every six months

[2] Strictly, deployment frequency is the reciprocal of batch size—the more frequently we deploy, the smaller the size of the batch. For more on measuring batch size in the context of IT service management, see Forsgren and Humble (2016).

Delivery lead times and deployment frequency are both measures of software delivery performance *tempo*. However, we wanted to investigate whether teams who improved their performance were doing so at the expense of the stability of the systems they were working on. Traditionally, reliability is measured as time between failures. However, in modern software products and services, which are rapidly changing complex systems, failure is inevitable, so the key question becomes: How quickly can service be restored? We asked respondents how long it generally takes to restore service for the primary application or service they work on when a service incident (e.g., unplanned outage, service impairment) occurs, offering the same options as for lead time (above).

Finally, a key metric when making changes to systems is what percentage of changes to production (including, for example, software releases and infrastructure configuration changes) fail. In the context of Lean, this is the same as percent complete and accurate for the product delivery process, and is a key quality metric. We asked respondents what percentage of changes for the primary application or service they work on either result in degraded service or subsequently require remediation (e.g., lead to service impairment or outage, require a hotfix, a rollback, a fix-forward, or a patch). The four measures selected are shown in Figure 2.1.

Software Delivery Performance
Lead Time
Deployment Frequency
Mean Time to Restore (MTTR)
Change Fail Percentage

Figure 2.1: Software Delivery Performance

In order to analyze delivery performance across the cohort we surveyed, we used a technique called *cluster analysis*. Cluster analysis is a foundational technique in statistical data analysis that attempts to group responses so that responses in the same group are more similar to each other than to responses in other groups. Each measurement is put on a separate dimension, and the clustering algorithm attempts to minimize the distance between all cluster members and maximize differences between clusters. This technique has no understanding of the semantics of responses—in other words, it doesn't know what counts as a "good" or "bad" response for any of the measures.[3]

This data-driven approach that categorizes the data without any bias toward "good" or "bad" gives us an opportunity to view trends in the industry without biasing the results a priori. Using cluster analysis also allowed us to identify categories of software delivery performance seen in the industry: Are there high performers and low performers, and what characteristics do they have?

We applied cluster analysis in all four years of the research project and found that every year, there were significantly different categories of software delivery performance in the industry. We also found that all four measures of software delivery performance are good classifiers and that the groups we identified in the analysis—high, medium, and low performers—were all significantly different across all four measures.

Tables 2.2 and 2.3 show you the details for software delivery performance for the last two years of our research (2016 and 2017).

[3] For more on cluster analysis, see Appendix B.

Table 2.2 Software Delivery Performance for 2016

2016	High Performers	Medium Performers	Low Performers
Deployment Frequency	On demand (multiple deploys per day)	Between once per week and once per month	Between once per month and once every six months
Lead Time for Changes	Less than one hour	Between one week and one month	Between one month and six months
MTTR	Less than one hour	Less than one day	Less than one day*
Change Failure Rate	0–15%	31–45%	16–30%

Table 2.3 Software Delivery Performance for 2017

2017	High Performers	Medium Performers	Low Performers
Deployment Frequency	On demand (multiple deploys per day)	Between once per week and once per month	Between once per week and once per month*
Lead Time for Changes	Less than one hour	Between one week and one month	Between one week and one month*
MTTR	Less than one hour	Less than one day	Between one day and one week
Change Failure Rate	0–15%	0–15%	31–45%

* Low performers were lower on average (at a statistically significant level) but had the same median as the medium performers.

Astonishingly, these results demonstrate that there is no trade-off between improving performance and achieving higher levels of stability and quality. Rather, high performers do better at *all* of these measures. This is precisely what the Agile and Lean movements predict, but much dogma in our industry still rests on the false assumption that moving faster means *trading off* against other performance goals, rather than enabling and reinforcing them.[4]

Furthermore, over the last few years we've found that the high-performing cluster is pulling away from the pack. The DevOps mantra of continuous improvement is both exciting and real, pushing companies to be their best, and leaving behind those who do not improve. Clearly, what was state of the art three years ago is just not good enough for today's business environment.

Compared to 2016, high performers in 2017 maintained or improved their performance, consistently maximizing both tempo and stability. Low performers, on the other hand, maintained the same level of throughput from 2014–2016 and only started to increase in 2017—likely realizing that the rest of the industry was pulling away from them. In 2017, we saw low performers lose some ground in stability. We suspect this is due to attempts to increase tempo ("work harder!") which fail to address the underlying obstacles to improved overall performance (for example, rearchitecture, process improvement, and automation). We show the trends in Figures 2.2 and 2.3.

---

[4] See https://continuousdelivery.com/2016/04/the-flaw-at-the-heart-of-bimodal-it/ for an analysis of problems with the bimodal approach to ITSM, which rests on this false assumption.

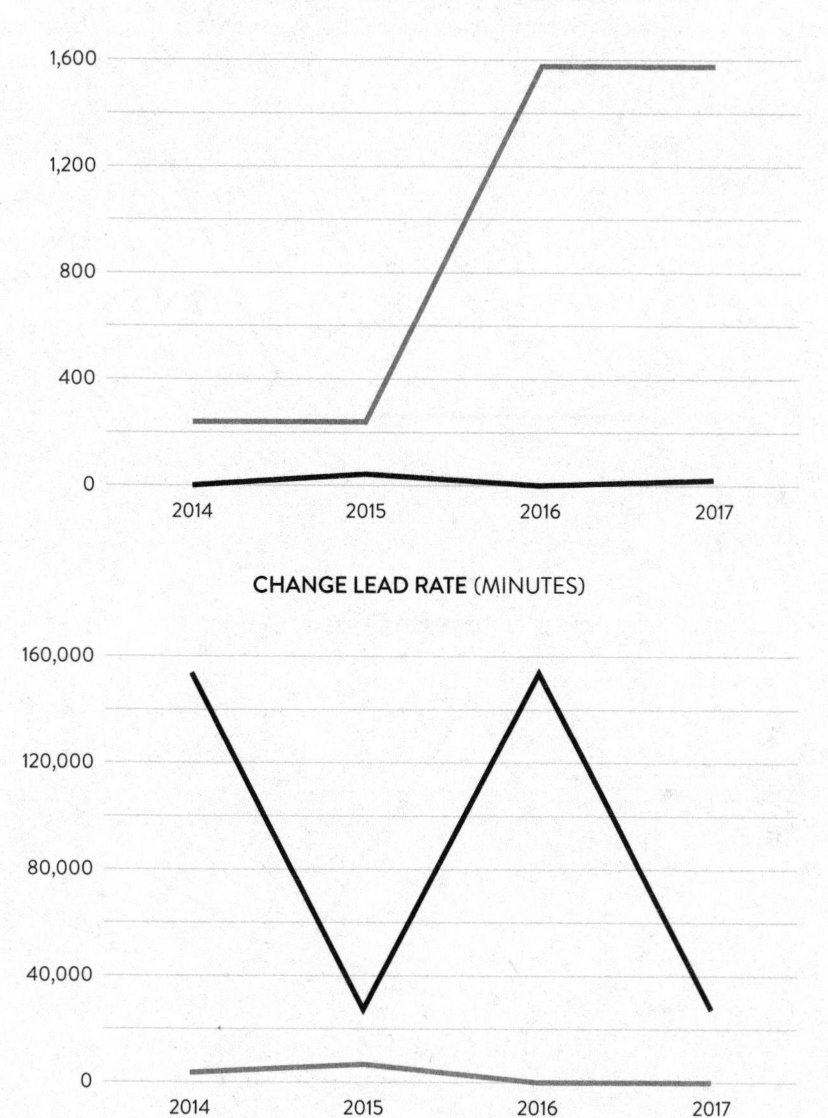

Figure 2.2: Year over Year Trends: Tempo

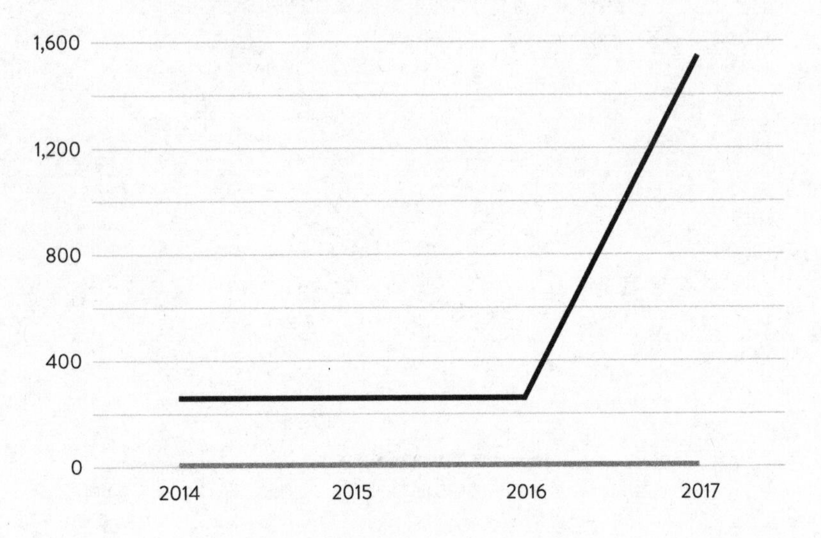

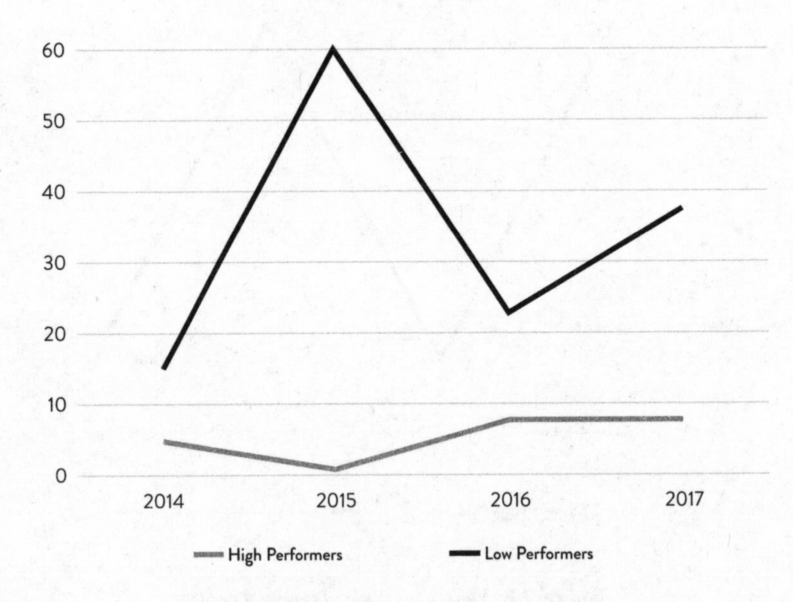

Figure 2.3: Year over Year Trends: Stability

Surprise!

Observant readers will notice that medium performers do worse than low performers on change fail rate in 2016. 2016 is the first year of our research where we see slightly inconsistent performance across our measures in any of our performance groups, and we see it in medium and low performers. Our research doesn't conclusively explain this, but we have a few ideas about why this might be the case.

One possible explanation is that medium performers are working along their technology transformation journey and dealing with the challenges that come from large-scale rearchitecture work, such as transitioning legacy code bases. This would also match another piece of the data from the 2016 study, where we found that medium performers spend more time on unplanned rework than low performers—because they report spending a greater proportion of time on new work.

We believe this new work could be occurring at the expense of ignoring critical rework, thus racking up technical debt which in turn leads to more fragile systems and, therefore, a higher change fail rate.

We have found a valid, reliable way to measure software delivery performance that satisfies the requirements we laid out. It focuses on global, system-level goals, and measures outcomes that different functions must collaborate in order to improve. The next question we wanted to answer is: Does software delivery performance matter?

THE IMPACT OF DELIVERY PERFORMANCE ON ORGANIZATIONAL PERFORMANCE

In order to measure organizational performance, survey respondents were asked to rate their organization's relative performance across several dimensions: profitability, market share, and productivity. This is a scale that has been validated multiple times in prior research (Widener 2007). This measure of organizational performance has also been found to be highly correlated to measures of return on investment (ROI), and it is robust to economic cycles—a great measure for our purposes. Analysis over several years shows that high-performing organizations were consistently *twice as likely* to exceed these goals as low performers. This demonstrates that your organization's software delivery capability can in fact provide a competitive advantage to your business.

In 2017, our research also explored how IT performance affects an organization's ability to achieve broader organizational goals—that is, goals that go beyond simple profit and revenue measures. Whether you're trying to generate profits or not, any organization today depends on technology to achieve its mission and provide value to its customers or stakeholders quickly, reliably, and securely. Whatever the mission, how a technology organization performs can predict overall organizational performance. To measure noncommercial goals, we used a scale that has been validated multiple times and is particularly well-suited for this purpose (Cavalluzzo and Ittner 2004). We found that high performers were also twice as likely to exceed objectives in quantity of goods and services, operating efficiency, customer satisfaction, quality of products or services, and achieving organization or mission goals. We show this relationship in Figure 2.4.

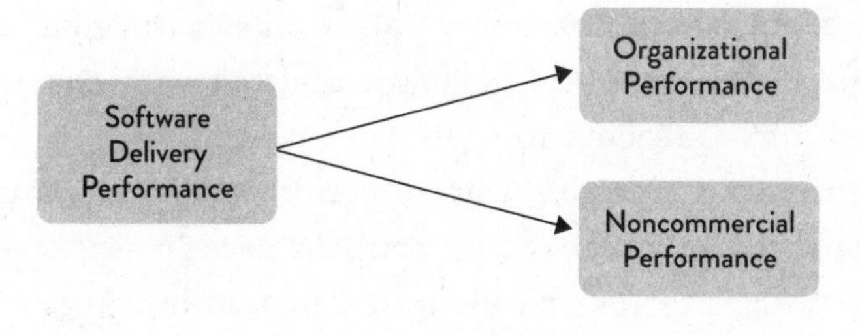

Figure 2.4: Impacts of Software Delivery Performance

Reading the Figures in This Book

We will include figures to help guide you through the research.

- When you see a box, this is a construct we have measured. (For details on constructs, see Chapter 13.)
- When you see an arrow linking boxes, this signifies a predictive relationship. You read that right: the research in this book includes analyses that go beyond correlation into prediction. (For details, see Chapter 12 on inferential prediction.) You can read these arrows using the words "drives," "predicts," "affects," or "impacts." These are all positive relationships unless otherwise noted.

For example, Figure 2.4 could be read as "software delivery performance impacts organizational performance and noncommercial performance."

In software organizations, the ability to work and deliver in small batches is especially important, because it allows you to gather user feedback quickly using techniques such as A/B testing.

It's worth noting that the ability to take an experimental approach to product development is highly correlated with the technical practices that contribute to continuous delivery.

The fact that software delivery performance matters provides a strong argument against outsourcing the development of software that is strategic to your business, and instead bringing this capability into the core of your organization. Even the US Federal Government, through initiatives such as the US Digital Service and its agency affiliates and the General Services Administration's Technology Transformation Service team, has invested in bringing software development capability in-house for strategic initiatives.

In contrast, most software used by businesses (such as office productivity software and payroll systems) are not strategic and should in many cases be acquired using the software-as-a-service model. Distinguishing which software is strategic and which isn't, and managing them appropriately, is of enormous importance. This topic is dealt with at length by Simon Wardley, creator of the Wardley mapping method (Wardley 2015).

DRIVING CHANGE

Now that we have defined software delivery performance in a way that is rigorous and measurable, we can make evidence-based decisions on how to improve the performance of teams building software-based products and services. We can compare and benchmark teams against the larger organizations they work in and against the wider industry. We can measure their improvement—or backsliding—over time. And perhaps most exciting of all, we can go beyond correlation and start testing prediction. We can test hypotheses about which practices—from managing work in process to test automation—actually impact delivery performance and the strength of these effects. We can measure other outcomes we care about, such as team burnout and deployment pain. We can answer questions like, "Do change management boards actually improve delivery performance?" (Spoiler alert: they do not; they are negatively correlated with tempo and stability.)

As we show in the next chapter, it is also possible to model and measure culture quantitatively. This enables us to measure the effect of DevOps and continuous delivery practices on culture and, in turn, the effect of culture on software delivery performance and organizational performance. Our ability to measure and reason about practices, culture, and outcomes is an incredibly powerful tool that can be used to great positive effect in the pursuit of ever higher performance.

You can, of course, use these tools to model your own performance. Use Table 2.3 to discover where in our taxonomy you fall. Use our measures for lead time, deployment frequency, time to restore service, and change fail rate, and ask your teams to set targets for these measures.

However, it is essential to use these tools carefully. In organizations with a learning culture, they are incredibly powerful. But "in pathological and bureaucratic organizational cultures, measurement is used as a form of control, and people hide information that challenges existing rules, strategies, and power structures. As Deming said, 'whenever there is fear, you get the wrong numbers'" (Humble et al. 2014, p. 56). Before you are ready to deploy a scientific approach to improving performance, you must first understand and develop your culture. It is to this topic we now turn.

CHAPTER 3

MEASURING AND CHANGING CULTURE

It is practically a truism in DevOps circles that culture is of huge importance. However, culture is intangible; there exist many definitions and models of culture. Our challenge was to find a model of culture that was well-defined in the scientific literature, could be measured effectively, and would have predictive power in our domain. Not only did we achieve these objectives, we also discovered that it is possible to influence and improve culture by implementing DevOps practices.

MODELING AND MEASURING CULTURE

There are many approaches to modeling *culture* in the literature. You can choose to look at national culture—for example, what country one belongs to. You may also talk about what organizational cultural values are enacted that influence the way teams behave. And even within organizational culture, there are several ways to define and model "culture." Organizational culture can exist at three levels in organizations: basic assumptions, values, and artifacts (Schein 1985). At the first level, basic assumptions are formed over time as members of a group or organization make sense of relationships, events, and activities. These interpretations are the least "visible" of the levels—and are the things that we just "know," and may find difficult to articulate, after we have been long enough in a team.

The second level of organizational culture are values, which are more "visible" to group members as these collective values and norms can be discussed and even debated by those who are aware of them. Values provide a lens through which group members view and interpret the relationships, events, and activities around them. Values also influence group interactions and activities by establishing social norms, which shape the actions of group members and provide contextual rules (Bansal 2003). These are quite often the "culture" we think of when we talk about the culture of a team and an organization.

The third level of organizational culture is the most visible and can be observed in artifacts. These artifacts can include written mission statements or creeds, technology, formal procedures, or even heroes and rituals (Pettigrew 1979).

Based on discussions in DevOps circles and the importance of "organizational culture" at the second level, we decided to select a model defined by sociologist Ron Westrum. Westrum had been researching human factors in system safety, particularly in the context of accidents in technological domains that were highly complex and risky, such as aviation and healthcare. In 1988, he developed a typology of organizational cultures (Westrum 2014):

- **Pathological** (power-oriented) organizations are characterized by large amounts of fear and threat. People often hoard information or withhold it for political reasons, or distort it to make themselves look better.

- **Bureaucratic** (rule-oriented) organizations protect departments. Those in the department want to maintain their "turf," insist on their own rules, and generally do things by the book—*their* book.
- **Generative** (performance-oriented) organizations focus on the mission. How do we accomplish our goal? Everything is subordinated to good performance, to doing what we are supposed to do.

Westrum's further insight was that the organizational culture predicts the way information flows through an organization. Westrum provides three characteristics of good information:

1. It provides answers to the questions that the receiver needs answered.
2. It is timely.
3. It is presented in such a way that it can be effectively used by the receiver.

Good information flow is critical to the safe and effective operation of high-tempo and high-consequence environments, including technology organizations. Westrum describes the characteristics of organizations that fall into his three types in Table 3.1.

An additional insight from Westrum was that this definition of organizational culture predicts performance outcomes. We keyed in on this in particular, because we hear so often that culture is important in DevOps, and we were interested in understanding if culture could predict software delivery performance.

Table 3.1 Westrum's Typology of Organizational Culture

Pathological (Power-Oriented)	Bureaucratic (Rule-Oriented)	Generative (Performance-Oriented)
Low cooperation	Modest cooperation	High cooperation
Messengers "shot"	Messengers neglected	Messengers trained
Responsibilities shirked	Narrow responsibilities	Risks are shared
Bridging discouraged	Bridging tolerated	Bridging encouraged
Failure leads to scapegoating	Failure leads to justice	Failure leads to inquiry
Novelty crushed	Novelty leads to problems	Novelty implemented

MEASURING CULTURE

In order to measure the culture of organizations, we take advantage of the fact that these types form "points on a scale . . . a 'Westrum continuum'" (Westrum 2014). This makes it an excellent candidate for Likert-type questions. In psychometrics, the Likert scale is used to measure people's perceptions by asking them to rate how strongly they agree or disagree with a statement. When people answer a Likert-type question, we assign the answer a value on a scale from 1 to 7, where 1 means "Strongly disagree" and 7 means "Strongly agree."

For this approach to work, the statement must be worded strongly, so that people can strongly agree or disagree (or indeed feel neutral) about it. You can see a re-creation from the survey showing the statements we created from Westrum's model, along with the Likert scale, in Figure 3.1.

	Strongly disagree	Disagree	Somewhat disagree	Neither agree nor disagree	Somewhat agree	Agree	Strongly agree
Information is actively sought.	○	○	○	○	○	○	○
Messengers are not punished when they deliver news of failures or other bad news.	○	○	○	○	○	○	○
Responsibilities are shared.	○	○	○	○	○	○	○
Cross-functional collaboration is encouraged and rewarded.	○	○	○	○	○	○	○
Failure causes inquiry.	○	○	○	○	○	○	○
New ideas are welcomed.	○	○	○	○	○	○	○
Failures are treated primarily as opportunities to improve the system.	○	○	○	○	○	○	○

Figure 3.1: Likert-Type Questions for Measuring Culture

Once we have the responses to these questions from several people (often dozens or hundreds of people), we need to determine if our measure of organizational culture is valid and reliable from a statistical point of view. That is, we need to find out if the questions are being understood similarly by all people taking the survey and if, taken together, they are actually measuring organizational culture. If analyses using several statistical tests confirm these properties, we call what we have measured a "construct" (in this case, our construct would be "Westrum organizational culture"), and we can then use this measure in further research.

Analyzing Constructs

Prior to conducting any analysis between our measures—for example, does organizational culture impact software delivery performance?—we must analyze the data and measures themselves. When using robust survey measures, we use *constructs.*

In this first step, we conducted several analyses to ensure our survey measures were valid and reliable. These analyses included tests for discriminant validity, convergent validity, and reliability.

- **Discriminant validity:** making sure that items that are not supposed to be related are actually unrelated (e.g., that items that we believe are not capturing organizational culture are not, in fact, related to it).
- **Convergent validity:** making sure that items that are supposed to be related are actually related (e.g., if measures are supposed to measure organizational culture, they do measure it).
- **Reliability:** making sure the items are read and interpreted similarly by those who take the survey. This is also referred to as internal consistency.

Taken together, validity and reliability analyses confirm our measures and come before any additional analyses to test for relationships, like correlation or prediction. For more on validity and reliability, refer to Chapter 13. Additional information about the statistical tests used to confirm validity and reliability can be found in Appendix C.

Our research has consistently found our Westrum construct—an indicator of the level of organizational culture that prioritizes trust and collaboration in the team—to be both valid and reliable.[1] This

[1] In 2016, 31% of respondents were classified as pathological, 48% bureaucratic, and 21% generative.

means you can use these questions in your surveys too. To calculate the "score" for each survey response, take the numerical value (1–7) corresponding to the answer to each question and calculate the mean across all questions. Then you can perform statistical analysis on the responses as a whole.

Culture enables information processing through three mechanisms. First, in organizations with a generative culture, people collaborate more effectively and there is a higher level of trust both across the organization and up and down the hierarchy. Second, "generative culture emphasizes the mission, an emphasis that allows people involved to put aside their personal issues and also the departmental issues that are so evident in bureaucratic organizations. The mission is primary. And third, generativity encourages a 'level playing field,' in which hierarchy plays less of a role" (Westrum 2014, p. 61).

We should emphasize that bureaucracy is not necessarily bad. As Mark Schwartz points out in *The Art of Business Value*, the goal of bureaucracy is to "ensure fairness by applying rules to administrative behavior. The rules would be the same for all cases—no one would receive preferential or discriminatory treatment. Not only that, but the rules would represent the best products of the accumulated knowledge of the organization: Formulated by bureaucrats who were experts in their fields, the rules would impose efficient structures and processes while guaranteeing fairness and eliminating arbitrariness" (Schwartz 2016, p. 56).

Westrum's description of a rule-oriented culture is perhaps best thought of as one where following the rules is considered more important than achieving the mission—and we have worked with teams in the US Federal Government we would have no issue describing as generative, as well as startups that are clearly pathological.

WHAT DOES WESTRUM ORGANIZATIONAL CULTURE PREDICT?

Westrum's theory posits that organizations with better information flow function more effectively. According to Westrum, this type of organizational culture has several important prerequisites, which means that it is a good proxy for the characteristics described by these prerequisites.

First, a good culture requires trust and cooperation between people across the organization, so it reflects the level of collaboration and trust inside the organization.

Second, better organizational culture can indicate higher quality decision-making. In a team with this type of culture, not only is better information available for making decisions, but those decisions are more easily reversed if they turn out to be wrong because the team is more likely to be open and transparent rather than closed and hierarchical.

Finally, teams with these cultural norms are likely to do a better job with their people, since problems are more rapidly discovered and addressed.

We hypothesized that culture would predict both software delivery performance and organizational performance. We also predicted that it would lead to higher levels of job satisfaction.[2] Both of these hypotheses proved to be true. We show these relationships in Figure 3.2.

---

[2] These hypotheses are based on previous research and existing theories, and bolstered by our own experiences and the experiences we see and hear from others in the industry. Our research hypotheses are all built this way. This is an example of inferential predictive research, which you can read more about in Chapter 12.

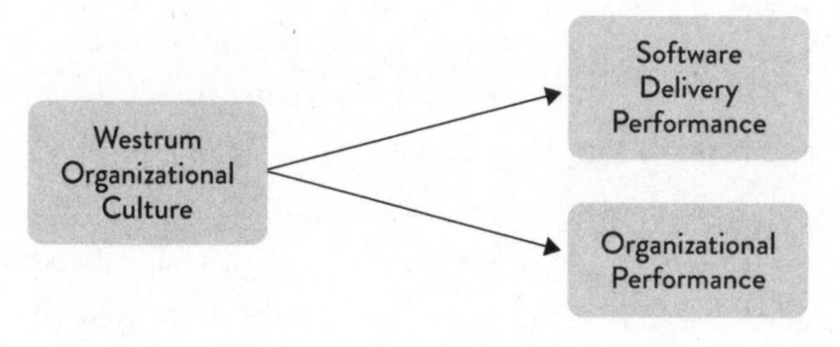

Figure 3.2: Westrum Organizational Culture's Outcomes

CONSEQUENCES OF WESTRUM'S THEORY FOR TECHNOLOGY ORGANIZATIONS

For modern organizations that hope to thrive in the face of increasingly rapid technological and economic change, both resilience and the ability to innovate through responding to this change are essential. Our research into the application of Westrum's theory to technology shows that these two characteristics are connected. Initially developed to predict safety outcomes, our research shows it also predicts both software delivery and organizational performance. This makes sense, because safety outcomes are performance outcomes in a healthcare setting. By extending this to technology, we expected this type of organizational culture to positively impact software delivery and organizational performance. This mirrors research performed by Google into how to create high-performing teams.

The Delivery Performance Construct

In Chapter 2, we said that delivery performance combines four metrics: lead time, release frequency, time to restore service, and change fail rate. When performing cluster analysis, all four metrics together meaningfully classify and discriminate among our high, medium, and low performers. That is, all four measures are good at categorizing teams. However, when we tried to turn these four metrics into a *construct*, we ran into a problem: the four measures don't pass all of the statistical tests of validity and reliability. Analysis showed that only lead time, release frequency, and time to restore together form a valid and reliable construct. Thus, in the rest of book, when we talk about *software delivery performance* it is defined using only the combination of those three metrics. Also, when software delivery performance is shown to correlate with some other construct, or when we talk about predictions involving software delivery performance, we're only talking about the construct as defined and measured this way.

Note, however, that change fail rate is strongly correlated with the software delivery performance construct, which means that in most cases, things correlated with the software delivery performance construct are also correlated with change fail rate.

Google wanted to discover if there were any common factors among its best-performing teams. They started a two-year research project to investigate what made Google teams effective, conducting "200+ interviews with . . . employees and [looking] at more than 250 attributes of 180+ active Google teams" (Google 2015). They expected to find a combination of individual traits and skills that would be key ingredients of high-performing teams. What they found instead was that "who is on a team matters less than how the team members interact, structure their work, and view their contributions" (Google 2015). In other words, it all comes down to team dynamics.

How organizations deal with failures or accidents is particularly instructive. Pathological organizations look for a "throat to choke": Investigations aim to find the person or persons "responsible" for the problem, and then punish or blame them. But in complex adaptive systems, accidents are almost never the fault of a single person who saw clearly what was going to happen and then ran toward it or failed to act to prevent it. Rather, accidents typically emerge from a complex interplay of contributing factors. Failure in complex systems is, like other types of behavior in such systems, emergent (Perrow 2011).

Thus, accident investigations that stop at "human error" are not just bad but dangerous. Human error should, instead, be the *start* of the investigation. Our goal should be to discover how we could improve information flow so that people have better or more timely information, or to find better tools to help prevent catastrophic failures following apparently mundane operations.

HOW DO WE CHANGE CULTURE?

John Shook, describing his experiences transforming the culture of the teams at the Fremont, California, car manufacturing plant that was the genesis of the Lean manufacturing movement in the US, wrote, "what my . . . experience taught me that was so powerful was that the way to change culture is not to first change how people think, but instead to start by changing how people behave—what they do" (Shook 2010).[3]

Thus we hypothesize that, following the theory developed by the Lean and Agile movements, implementing the practices of these movements can have an effect on culture. We set out to

[3] The story of this transformation is told in episode 561 of the WBEZ radio show *This American Life* (This American Life 2015).

look at both technical and management practices, and to measure their impact on culture. Our research shows that Lean management, along with a set of other technical practices known collectively as *continuous delivery* (Humble and Farley 2010), do in fact impact culture, as shown in Figure 3.3.

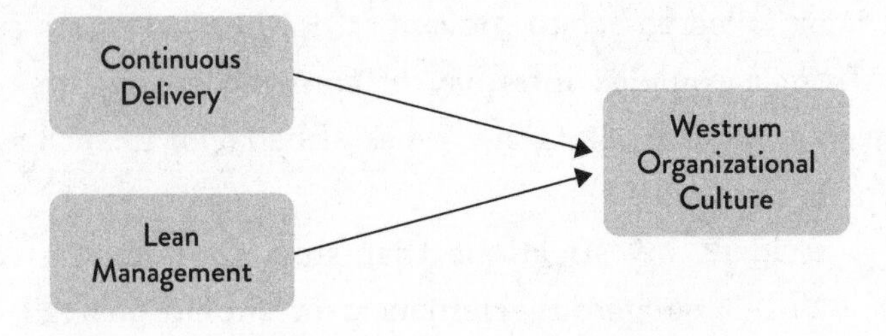

Figure 3.3: Westrum Organizational Culture's Drivers

You can act your way to a better culture by implementing these practices in technology organizations, just as you can in manufacturing. In the next chapter we'll examine the technical practices, and then in Chapters 7 and 8 we'll discuss management practices.

CHAPTER 4

TECHNICAL PRACTICES

At the time the Agile Manifesto was published in 2001, Extreme Programming (XP) was one of the most popular Agile frameworks.[1] In contrast to Scrum, XP prescribes a number of technical practices such as test-driven development and continuous integration. *Continuous Delivery* (Humble and Farley 2010) also emphasizes the importance of these technical practices (combined with comprehensive configuration management) as an enabler of more frequent, higher-quality, and lower-risk software releases.

Many Agile adoptions have treated technical practices as secondary compared to the management and team practices that some Agile frameworks emphasize. Our research shows that technical practices play a vital role in achieving these outcomes.

In this chapter, we discuss the research we performed to measure continuous delivery as a capability and to assess its impact on software delivery performance, organizational culture, and other outcome measures, such as team burnout and deployment pain. We find that continuous delivery practices do in fact have a measurable impact on these outcomes.

[1] According to Google Trends, Scrum overtook Extreme Programming around January 2006, and has continued to grow in popularity while Extreme Programming has flatlined.

WHAT IS CONTINUOUS DELIVERY?

Continuous delivery is a set of capabilities that enable us to get changes of all kinds—features, configuration changes, bug fixes, experiments—into production or into the hands of users *safely*, *quickly*, and *sustainably*. There are five key principles at the heart of continuous delivery:

- **Build quality in.** The third of W. Edwards Deming's fourteen points for management states, "Cease dependence on inspection to achieve quality. Eliminate the need for inspection on a mass basis by building quality into the product in the first place" (Deming 2000). In continuous delivery, we invest in building a culture supported by tools and people where we can detect any issues quickly, so that they can be fixed straight away when they are cheap to detect and resolve.
- **Work in small batches.** Organizations tend to plan work in big chunks—whether building new products or services or investing in organizational change. By splitting work up into much smaller chunks that deliver measurable business outcomes quickly for a small part of our target market, we get essential feedback on the work we are doing so that we can course correct. Even though working in small chunks adds some overhead, it reaps enormous rewards by allowing us to avoid work that delivers zero or negative value for our organizations.

  A key goal of continuous delivery is changing the economics of the software delivery process so the cost of pushing out individual changes is very low.

- **Computers perform repetitive tasks; people solve problems.** One important strategy to reduce the cost of pushing out changes is to take repetitive work that takes a long time, such as regression testing and software deployments, and invest in simplifying and automating this work. Thus, we free up people for higher-value problem-solving work, such as improving the design of our systems and processes in response to feedback.
- **Relentlessly pursue continuous improvement.** The most important characteristic of high-performing teams is that they are never satisfied: they always strive to get better. High performers make improvement part of everybody's daily work.
- **Everyone is responsible.** As we learned from Ron Westrum, in bureaucratic organizations teams tend to focus on departmental goals rather than organizational goals. Thus, development focuses on throughput, testing on quality, and operations on stability. However, in reality these are all system-level outcomes, and they can only be achieved by close collaboration between everyone involved in the software delivery process.

  A key objective for management is making the state of these system-level outcomes transparent, working with the rest of the organization to set measurable, achievable, time-bound goals for these outcomes, and then helping their teams work toward them.

In order to implement continuous delivery, we must create the following foundations:

- **Comprehensive configuration management.** It should be possible to provision our environments and build, test, and deploy our software in a fully automated fashion purely from information stored in version control. Any change to environments or the software that runs on them should be applied using an automated process from version control. This still leaves room for manual approvals—but once approved, all changes should be applied automatically.
- **Continuous integration (CI).** Many software development teams are used to developing features on branches for days or even weeks. Integrating all these branches requires significant time and rework. Following our principle of working in small batches and building quality in, high- performing teams keep branches short-lived (less than one day's work) and integrate them *into* trunk/master frequently. Each change triggers a build process that includes running unit tests. If any part of this process fails, developers fix it immediately.
- **Continuous testing.** Testing is not something that we should only start once a feature or a release is "dev complete." Because testing is so essential, we should be doing it all the time as an integral part of the development process. Automated unit and acceptance tests should be run against every commit to version control to give developers fast feedback on their changes. Developers should be able to run all automated tests on their workstations in order to triage and fix defects. Testers should be performing exploratory testing continuously against the latest builds to come out of CI. No one should be saying they are "done" with any work until all relevant automated tests have been written and are passing.

Implementing continuous delivery means creating multiple feedback loops to ensure that high-quality software gets delivered to users more frequently and more reliably.[2] When implemented correctly, the process of releasing new versions to users should be a routine activity that can be performed on demand at any time. Continuous delivery requires that developers and testers, as well as UX, product, and operations people, collaborate effectively throughout the delivery process.

THE IMPACT OF CONTINUOUS DELIVERY

In the first few iterations of our research from 2014–2016, we modeled and measured a number of capabilities:

- The use of version control for application code, system configuration, application configuration, and build and configuration scripts
- Comprehensive test automation that is reliable, easy to fix, and runs regularly
- Deployment automation
- Continuous integration
- Shifting left on security: bringing security—and security teams—in process with software delivery rather than as a downstream phase
- Using trunk-based development as opposed to long-lived feature branches
- Effective test data management

[2] The key pattern which connects these feedback loops is known as a *deployment pipeline*, see https://continuousdelivery.com/implementing/patterns/.

Most of these capabilities are measured in the form of constructs, using Likert-type questions.[3] For example, to measure the version control capability, we ask respondents to report, on a Likert scale, the extent to which they agree or disagree with the following statements:

- Our application code is in a version control system.
- Our system configurations are in a version control system.
- Our application configurations are in a version control system.
- Our scripts for automating build and configuration are in a version control system.

We then use statistical analysis to determine the extent to which these capabilities influence the outcomes we care about. As expected, when taken together, these capabilities have a strong positive impact on software delivery performance. (We discuss some of the nuances of how to implement these practices later in this chapter.) However, they also have other significant benefits: they help to decrease deployment pain and team burnout. While we have heard in the organizations we work with anecdotal evidence of these quality-of-work benefits for years, seeing evidence in the data was fantastic. And it makes sense: we expect this because when teams practice CD, deployment to production is not an enormous, big-bang event—it's something that can be done during normal business hours as a part of regular daily work. (We cover team health in more depth in Chapter 9.) Interestingly, teams that did well with continuous delivery also identified more strongly with the organization they worked for—a key predictor of organizational performance that we discuss in Chapter 10.

[3] A notable exception is deployment automation.

As discussed in Chapter 3, we hypothesized that implementing CD would influence organizational culture. Our analysis shows that this is indeed the case. If you want to improve your culture, implementing CD practices will help. By giving developers the tools to detect problems when they occur, the time and resources to invest in their development, and the authority to fix problems straight away, we create an environment where developers accept responsibility for global outcomes such as quality and stability. This has a positive influence on the group interactions and activities of team members' organizational environment and culture.

In 2017, we extended our analysis and were more explicit in how we measured the relationship between the technical capabilities that were important to CD. To do this, we created a first-order continuous delivery construct. That is, we measured CD directly, which gave us insights into a team's ability to achieve the following outcomes:

- Teams can deploy to production (or to end users) on demand, throughout the software delivery lifecycle.
- Fast feedback on the quality and deployability of the system is available to everyone on the team, and people make acting on this feedback their highest priority.

Our analysis showed that the original capabilities measured in 2014–2016 had a strong and statistically significant impact on these outcomes.[4] We also measured two new capabilities, which also turned out to have a strong and statistically significant impact on continuous delivery:

[4] Only a subset of technical capabilities was tested due to length limitations. See the diagram at the end of Appendix A for these capabilities.

- A loosely coupled, well-encapsulated architecture (this is discussed in more detail in Chapter 5)
- Teams that can choose their own tools based on what is best for the users of those tools

We show these relationships in Figure 4.1.

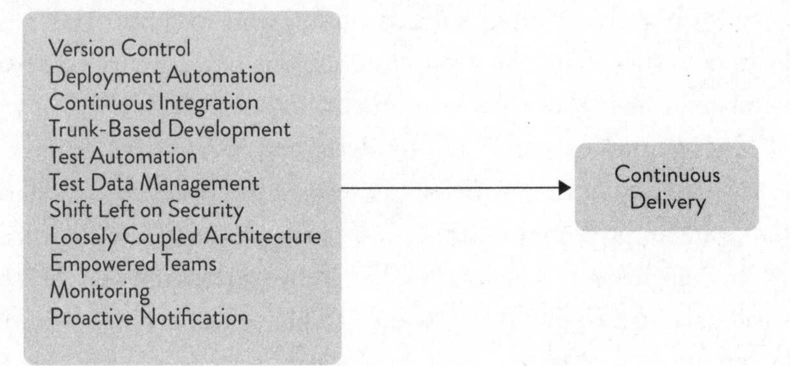

Figure 4.1: Drivers of Continuous Delivery

Since achieving continuous delivery for the sake of continuous delivery is not enough, we wanted to investigate its impacts on organizations. We hypothesized that it should drive performance improvements in software delivery, and prior research suggested it could even improve culture. As before, we found that teams that did well at continuous delivery achieved the following outcomes:

- Strong identification with the organization you work for (see Chapter 10)
- Higher levels of software delivery performance (lead time, deploy frequency, time to restore service)
- Lower change fail rates
- A generative, performance-oriented culture (see Chapter 3)

These relationships are shown in Figure 4.2.

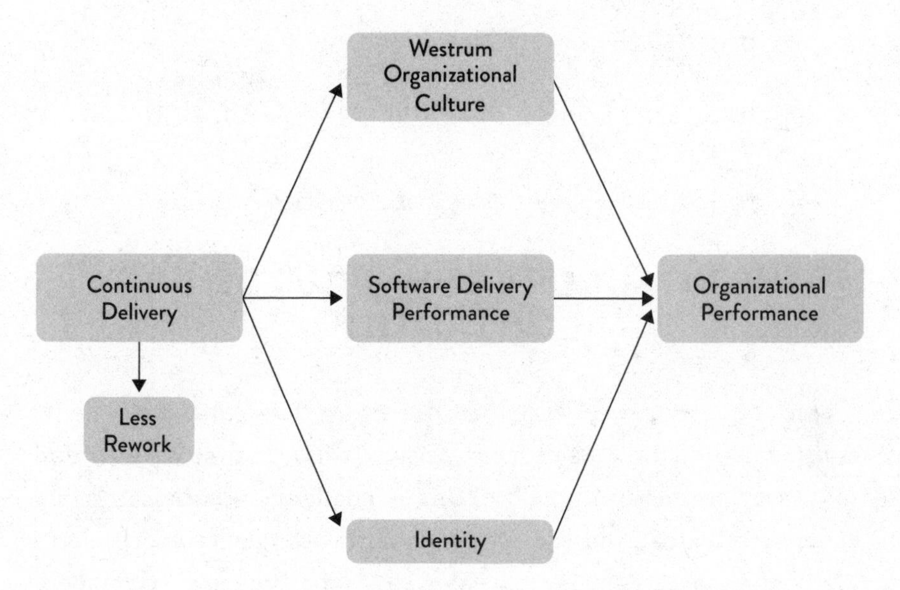

Figure 4.2: Impacts of Continuous Delivery

Even better, our research found that improvements in CD brought payoffs in the way that work *felt*. This means that investments in technology are also investments in people, and these investments will make our technology process more sustainable (Figure 4.3). Thus, CD helps us achieve one of the twelve principles of the Agile Manifesto: "Agile processes promote sustainable development. The sponsors, developers, and users should be able to maintain a constant pace indefinitely" (Beck et al. 2001).

- Lower levels of deployment pain
- Reduced team burnout (see Chapter 9)

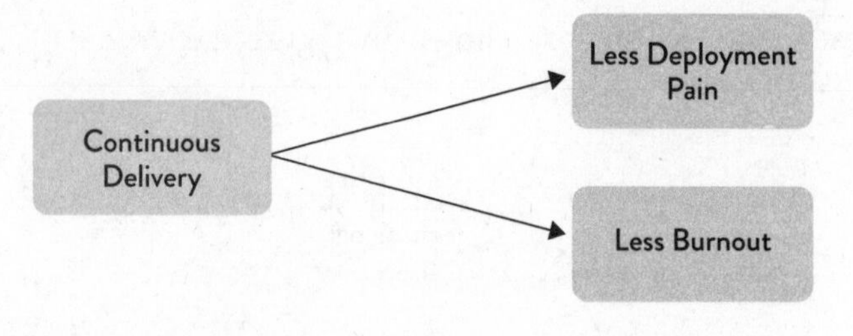

Figure 4.3: Continuous Delivery Makes Work More Sustainable

THE IMPACT OF CONTINUOUS DELIVERY ON QUALITY

A crucial question we wanted to address is: Does continuous delivery increase quality? In order to answer this, we first have to find some way to measure quality. This is challenging because quality is very contextual and subjective. As software quality expert Jerry Weinberg says, "Quality is value to some person" (Weinberg 1992, p. 7).

We already know that continuous delivery predicts lower change fail rates, which is an important quality metric. However, we also tested several additional proxy variables for quality:

- The quality and performance of applications, as perceived by those working on them
- The percentage of time spent on rework or unplanned work
- The percentage of time spent working on defects identified by end users

Our analysis found that all measures were correlated with software delivery performance. However, the strongest correlation was seen in the percentage of time spent on rework or unplanned work, including break/fix work, emergency software deployments and patches, responding to urgent audit documentation requests, and so forth. Furthermore, continuous delivery predicts lower levels of unplanned work and rework in a statistically significant way. We found that the amount of time spent on new work, unplanned work or rework, and other kinds of work, was significantly different between high performers and low performers. We show these differences in Figure 4.4.

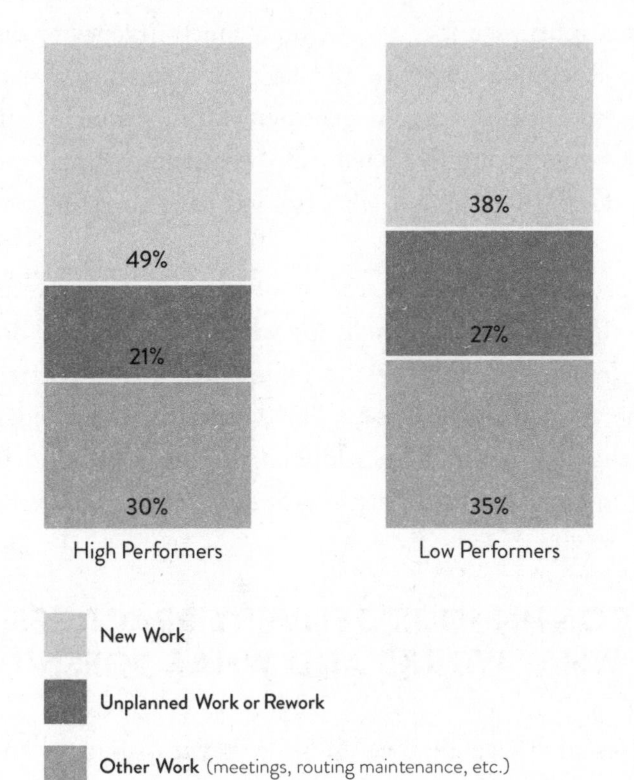

Figure 4.4: New Work vs. Unplanned Work

High performers reported spending 49% of their time on new work and 21% on unplanned work or rework. In contrast, low performers spend 38% of their time on new work and 27% on unplanned work or rework.

Unplanned work and rework are useful proxies for quality because they represent a failure to build quality into our products. In *The Visible Ops Handbook*, unplanned work is described as the difference between "paying attention to the low fuel warning light on an automobile versus running out of gas on the highway" (Behr et al. 2004). In the first case, the organization can fix the problem in a planned manner, without much urgency or disruption to other scheduled work. In the second case, they must fix the problem in a highly urgent manner, often requiring all hands on deck—for example, have six engineers drop everything and run down the highway with full gas cans to refuel a stranded truck.

Similarly, John Seddon, creator of the Vanguard Method, emphasizes the importance of reducing what he calls failure demand—demand for work caused by the failure to do the right thing the first time by improving the quality of service we provide. This is one of the key goals of continuous delivery, with its focus on working in small batches with continuous in-process testing.

CONTINUOUS DELIVERY PRACTICES: WHAT WORKS AND WHAT DOESN'T

In our research, we discovered nine key capabilities that drive continuous delivery, listed earlier in this chapter. Some of these capabilities have interesting nuances which we'll discuss in this section—with the exception of architecture and tool choice, which get a whole chapter to themselves (Chapter 5). Continuous integration and deployment automation are not discussed further in this chapter.

VERSION CONTROL

The comprehensive use of version control is relatively uncontroversial. We asked if respondents were keeping application code, system configuration, application configuration, and scripts for automating build and configuration in version control. These factors together predict IT performance and form a key component of continuous delivery. What was most interesting was that keeping system and application configuration in version control was more highly correlated with software delivery performance than keeping application code in version control. Configuration is normally considered a secondary concern to application code in configuration management, but our research shows that this is a misconception.

TEST AUTOMATION

As discussed above, test automation is a key part of continuous delivery. Based on our analysis, the following practices predict IT performance:

- Having automated tests that are *reliable*: when the automated tests pass, teams are confident that their software is releasable. Furthermore, they are confident that test failures indicate a real defect. Too many test suites are flaky and unreliable, producing false positives and negatives—it's worth investing ongoing effort into a suite that is reliable.

One way to achieve this is to put automated tests that are not reliable in a separate *quarantine suite* that is run independently.[5] Or, of course, you could just delete them. If they're version-controlled (as they should be), you can always get them back.

- Developers primarily create and maintain acceptance tests, and they can easily reproduce and fix them on their development workstations. It's interesting to note that having automated tests primarily created and maintained either by QA or an outsourced party is not correlated with IT performance. The theory behind this is that when developers are involved in creating and maintaining acceptance tests, there are two important effects. First, the code becomes more testable when developers write tests. This is one of the main reasons why test-driven development (TDD) is an important practice—it forces developers to create more testable designs. Second, when developers are responsible for the automated tests, they care more about them and will invest more effort into maintaining and fixing them.

None of this means that we should be getting rid of testers. Testers serve an essential role in the software delivery lifecycle, performing manual testing such as exploratory, usability, and acceptance testing, and helping to create and evolve suites of automated tests by working alongside developers.

Once you have these automated tests, our analysis shows it's important to run them regularly. Every commit should trigger a build of the software and running a set of fast, automated tests.

5 For more information, see https://martinfowler.com/articles/nonDeterminism.html.

Developers should get feedback from a more comprehensive suite of acceptance and performance tests every day. Furthermore, current builds should be available to testers for exploratory testing.

TEST DATA MANAGEMENT

When creating automated tests, managing test data can be hard. In our data, successful teams had adequate test data to run their fully automated test suites and could acquire test data for running automated tests on demand. In addition, test data was not a limit on the automated tests they could run.

TRUNK-BASED DEVELOPMENT

Our research also found that developing off trunk/master rather than on long-lived feature branches was correlated with higher delivery performance. Teams that did well had fewer than three active branches at any time, their branches had very short lifetimes (less than a day) before being merged into trunk and never had "code freeze" or stabilization periods. It's worth re-emphasizing that these results are independent of team size, organization size, or industry.

Even after finding that trunk-based development practices contribute to better software delivery performance, some developers who are used to the "GitHub Flow" workflow[6] remain skeptical. This workflow relies heavily on developing with branches and only periodically merging to trunk. We have heard, for example, that branching strategies are effective if development teams don't

[6] For a description of GitHub Flow, see https://guides.github.com/introduction/flow/.

maintain branches for too long—and we agree that working on short-lived branches that are merged into trunk at least daily is consistent with commonly accepted continuous integration practices.

We conducted additional research and found that teams using branches that live a short amount of time (integration times less than a day) combined with short merging and integration periods (less than a day) do better in terms of software delivery performance than teams using longer-lived branches. Anecdotally, and based on our own experience, we hypothesize that this is because having multiple long-lived branches discourages both refactoring and intrateam communication. We should note, however, that GitHub Flow *is* suitable for open source projects whose contributors are not working on a project full time. In that situation, it makes sense for branches that part-time contributors are working on to live for longer periods of time without being merged.

INFORMATION SECURITY

High-performing teams were more likely to incorporate information security into the delivery process. Their infosec personnel provided feedback at every step of the software delivery lifecycle, from design through demos to helping with test automation. However, they did so in a way that did not slow down the development process, integrating security concerns into the daily work of teams. In fact, integrating these security practices contributed to software delivery performance.

ADOPTING CONTINUOUS DELIVERY

Our research shows that the technical practices of continuous delivery have a huge impact on many aspects of an organization. Continuous delivery improves both delivery performance and quality, and also helps improve culture and reduce burnout and deployment pain. However, implementing these practices often requires rethinking everything—from how teams work, to how they interact with each other, to what tools and processes they use. It also requires substantial investment in test and deployment automation, combined with relentless work to simplify systems architecture on an ongoing basis to ensure that this automation isn't prohibitively expensive to create and maintain.

Thus, a critical obstacle to implementing continuous delivery is enterprise and application architecture. We'll discuss the results of our research into this important topic in Chapter 5.

CHAPTER 5

ARCHITECTURE

We've seen that adopting continuous delivery practices improves delivery performance, impacts culture, and reduces burnout and deployment pain. However, the architecture of your software and the services it depends on can be a significant barrier to increasing both the tempo and stability of the release process and the systems delivered.

Furthermore, DevOps and continuous delivery originated in web-based systems, so it's legitimate to ask if they can be applied to mainframe systems, firmware, or to an average big-ball-of-mud enterprise environment (Foote and Yoder 1997) consisting of thousands of tightly coupled systems.

We set out to discover the impact of architectural decisions and constraints on delivery performance, and what makes an effective architecture. We found that high performance is possible with all kinds of systems, provided that systems—and the teams that build and maintain them—are loosely coupled.

This key architectural property enables teams to easily test and deploy individual components or services even as the organization and the number of systems it operates grow—that is, it allows organizations to increase their productivity as they scale.

TYPES OF SYSTEMS AND DELIVERY PERFORMANCE

We examined a large number of types of systems to discover if there was a correlation between the type of system and team performance. We looked at the following types of systems, both as the primary system under development and as a service being integrated against:

- Greenfield: new systems that have not yet been released
- Systems of engagement (used directly by end users)
- Systems of record (used to store business-critical information where data consistency and integrity is critical)
- Custom software developed by another company
- Custom software developed in-house
- Packaged, commercial off-the-shelf software
- Embedded software that runs on a manufactured hardware device
- Software with a user-installed component (including mobile apps)
- Non-mainframe software that runs on servers operated by another company
- Non-mainframe software that runs on our own servers
- Mainframe software

We discovered that low performers were more likely to say that the software they were building—or the set of services they had to interact with—was custom software developed by another company (e.g., an outsourcing partner). Low performers were also more likely to be working on mainframe systems. Interestingly, having to integrate *against* mainframe systems was not significantly correlated with performance.

In the rest of the cases, there was no significant correlation between system type and delivery performance. We found this surprising: we had expected teams working on packaged software, systems of record, or embedded systems to perform worse, and teams working on systems of engagement and greenfield systems to perform better. The data shows that this is not the case.

This reinforces the importance of focusing on the architectural *characteristics*, discussed below, rather than the implementation details of your architecture. It's possible to achieve these characteristics even with packaged software and "legacy" mainframe systems—and, conversely, employing the latest whizzy microservices architecture deployed on containers is no guarantee of higher performance if you ignore these characteristics.

As we said in Chapter 2, given that software delivery performance impacts organizational performance, it's important to invest in your capabilities to create and evolve the core, strategic software products and services that provide a key differentiator for your business. The fact that low performers were more likely to be using—or integrating against—custom software developed by another company underlines the importance of bringing this capability in-house.

FOCUS ON DEPLOYABILITY AND TESTABILITY

Although in most cases the type of system you are building is not important in terms of achieving high performance, two architectural *characteristics* are. Those who agreed with the following statements were more likely to be in the high-performing group:

- We can do most of our testing without requiring an integrated environment.[1]
- We can and do deploy or release our application independently of other applications/services it depends on.

It appears that these *characteristics* of architectural decisions, which we refer to as testability and deployability, are important in creating high performance. To achieve these characteristics, design systems are loosely coupled—that is, can be changed and validated independently of each other. In the 2017 survey, we expanded our analysis to test the extent to which a loosely coupled, well-encapsulated architecture drives IT performance. We discovered that it does; indeed, the biggest contributor to continuous delivery in the 2017 analysis—larger even than test and deployment automation—is whether teams can:

- Make large-scale changes to the design of their system without the permission of somebody outside the team
- Make large-scale changes to the design of their system without depending on other teams to make changes in their systems or creating significant work for other teams
- Complete their work without communicating and coordinating with people outside their team
- Deploy and release their product or service on demand, regardless of other services it depends upon
- Do most of their testing on demand, without requiring an integrated test environment
- Perform deployments during normal business hours with negligible downtime

[1] We define an integrated environment as one in which multiple independent services are deployed together, such as a staging environment. In many enterprises, integrated environments are expensive and require significant set-up time.

In teams which scored highly on architectural capabilities, little communication is required between delivery teams to get their work done, and the architecture of the system is designed to enable teams to test, deploy, and change their systems without dependencies on other teams. In other words, architecture and teams are loosely coupled. To enable this, we must also ensure delivery teams are cross-functional, with all the skills necessary to design, develop, test, deploy, and operate the system on the same team.

This connection between communication bandwidth and systems architecture was first discussed by Melvin Conway, who said, "organizations which design systems . . . are constrained to produce designs which are copies of the communication structures of these organizations" (Conway 1968). Our research lends support to what is sometimes called the "inverse Conway Maneuver,"[2] which states that organizations should evolve their team and organizational structure to achieve the desired architecture. The goal is for your architecture to support the ability of teams to get their work done—from design through to deployment—without requiring high-bandwidth communication between teams.

Architectural approaches that enable this strategy include the use of bounded contexts and APIs as a way to decouple large domains into smaller, more loosely coupled units, and the use of test doubles and virtualization as a way to test services or components in isolation. Service-oriented architectures are supposed to enable these outcomes, as should any true microservices architecture. However, it's essential to be very strict about these outcomes when implementing such architectures. Unfortunately, in real life, many

[2] See https://www.thoughtworks.com/radar/techniques/inverse-conway-maneuver for more information.

so-called service-oriented architectures don't permit testing and deploying services independently of each other, and thus will not enable teams to achieve higher performance.[3]

Of course DevOps is all about better collaboration between teams, and we don't mean to suggest teams shouldn't work together. The goal of a loosely coupled architecture is to ensure that the available communication bandwidth isn't overwhelmed by fine-grained decision-making at the implementation level, so we can instead use that bandwidth for discussing higher-level shared goals and how to achieve them.

A LOOSELY COUPLED ARCHITECTURE ENABLES SCALING

If we achieve a loosely coupled, well-encapsulated architecture with an organizational structure to match, two important things happen. First, we can achieve better delivery performance, increasing both tempo and stability while reducing the burnout and the pain of deployment. Second, we can substantially grow the size of our engineering organization and increase productivity linearly—or better than linearly—as we do so.

To measure productivity, we calculated the following metric from our data: number of deploys per day per developer. The orthodox view of scaling software development teams states that while adding developers to a team may increase overall productivity, individual developer productivity will in fact decrease due to communication and integration overheads. However, when looking at number of deploys per day per developer for respondents who deploy at least once per day, we see the results plotted in Figure 5.1.

---

[3] Steve Yegge's "platform rant" contains some excellent advice on achieving these goals: http://bit.ly/yegge-platform-rant.

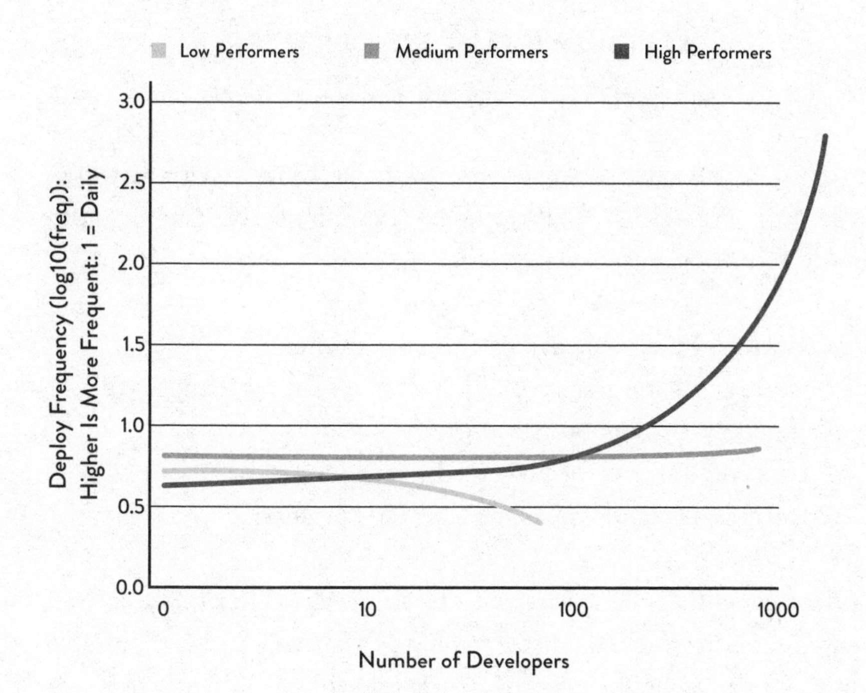

Figure 5.1: Deploys per Developer per Day

As the number of developers increases, we found:

- Low performers deploy with decreasing frequency.
- Medium performers deploy at a constant frequency.
- High performers deploy at a significantly increasing frequency.

By focusing on the factors that predict high delivery performance—a goal-oriented generative culture, a modular architecture, engineering practices that enable continuous delivery, and effective leadership—we can scale deployments per developer per day linearly or better with the number of developers. This allows our business to move *faster* as we add more people, not slow down, as is more typically the case.

ALLOW TEAMS TO CHOOSE THEIR OWN TOOLS

In many organizations, engineers must use tools and frameworks from an approved list. This approach typically serves one or more of the following purposes:

- Reducing the complexity of the environment
- Ensuring the necessary skills are in place to manage the technology throughout its lifecycle
- Increasing purchasing power with vendors
- Ensuring all technologies are correctly licensed

However, there is a downside to this lack of flexibility: it prevents teams from choosing technologies that will be most suitable for their particular needs, and from experimenting with new approaches and paradigms to solve their problems.

Our analysis shows that tool choice is an important piece of technical work. When teams can decide which tools they use, it contributes to software delivery performance and, in turn, to organizational performance. This isn't surprising. The technical professionals who develop and deliver software and run complex infrastructures make these tool choices based on what is best for completing their work and supporting their users. Similar results have been found in other studies of technical professionals (e.g., Forsgren et al. 2016), suggesting that the upsides of delegating tool choice to teams may outweigh the disadvantages.

That said, there is a place for standardization, particularly around the architecture and configuration of infrastructure. The benefits of a standardized operational platform are discussed at length by Humble (2017). Another example is Steve Yegge's description of Amazon's move to an SOA, in which he notes, "Debugging problems with someone else's code gets a LOT harder, and is basically impossible unless there is a universal standard way to run every service in a debuggable sandbox" (Yegge 2011).

Another finding in our research is that teams that build security into their work also do better at continuous delivery. A key element of this is ensuring that information security teams make pre-approved, easy-to-consume libraries, packages, toolchains, and processes available for developers and IT operations to use in their work.

There is no contradiction here. When the tools provided actually make life easier for the engineers who use them, they will adopt them of their own free will. This is a much better approach than forcing them to use tools that have been chosen for the convenience of other stakeholders. A focus on usability and customer satisfaction is as important when choosing or building tools for internal customers as it is when building products for external customers, and allowing your engineers to choose whether or not to use them ensures that we keep ourselves honest in this respect.

ARCHITECTS SHOULD FOCUS ON ENGINEERS AND OUTCOMES, NOT TOOLS OR TECHNOLOGIES

Discussions around architecture often focus on tools and technologies. Should the organization adopt microservices or serverless architectures? Should they use Kubernetes or Mesos? Which CI server, language, or framework should they standardize on? Our research shows that these are wrong questions to focus on.

What tools or technologies you use is irrelevant if the people who must use them hate using them, or if they don't achieve the outcomes and enable the behaviors we care about. What is important is enabling teams to make changes to their products or services without depending on other teams or systems. Architects should collaborate closely with their users—the engineers who build and operate the systems through which the organization achieves its mission—to help them achieve better outcomes and provide them the tools and technologies that will enable these outcomes.

CHAPTER 6

INTEGRATING INFOSEC INTO THE DELIVERY LIFECYCLE

Arguably the DevOps movement is poorly named—ignoring functions such as testing, product management, and information security. The original intent of the DevOps movement was—in part—to bring together developers and operations teams to create win-win solutions in the pursuit of system-level goals, rather than throwing work over the wall and pointing fingers when things went wrong. However, this kind of behavior is not limited to just development and operations, it occurs wherever different functions within the software delivery value stream do not work effectively together.

This is particularly true when discussing the role of information security teams. Infosec is a vitally important function in an era where threats are ubiquitous and ongoing. However, infosec teams are often poorly staffed—James Wickett, Head of Research at Signal Sciences, cites a ratio of 1 infosec person per 10 infrastructure people per 100 developers in large companies (Wickett 2014)—and they are usually only involved at the end of the software delivery lifecycle when it is often painful and expensive to make changes necessary to improve security. Furthermore, many developers are ignorant of common security risks, such as the OWASP Top 10,[1] and how to prevent them.

[1] For more information, see https://www.owasp.org/index.php/Category:OWASP_Top_Ten_Project.

Our research shows that building security into software development not only improves delivery performance but also improves security quality. Organizations with high delivery performance spend significantly less time remediating security issues.

SHIFTING LEFT ON SECURITY

We found that when teams "shift left" on information security—that is, when they build it into the software delivery process instead of making it a separate phase that happens downstream of the development process—this positively impacts their ability to practice continuous delivery. This, in turn, positively impacts delivery performance.

What does "shifting left" entail? First, security reviews are conducted for all major features, and this review process is performed in such a way that it doesn't slow down the development process. How can we ensure that paying attention to security doesn't reduce development throughput? This is the focus of the second aspect of this capability: information security should be integrated into the entire software delivery lifecycle from development through operations. This means infosec experts should contribute to the process of designing applications, attend and provide feedback on demonstrations of the software, and ensure that security features are tested as part of the automated test suite. Finally, we want to make it easy for developers to do the right thing when it comes to infosec. This can be achieved by ensuring that there are easy-to-consume, preapproved libraries, packages, toolchains, and processes available for developers and IT operations.

What we see here is a shift from information security teams doing the security reviews themselves to giving the developers the means to build security in. This reflects two realities: First, it's much easier to make sure that the people building the software are doing the right thing than inspect nearly completed systems and features to find significant architectural problems and defects that involve a substantial rework. Second, information security teams simply don't have the capacity to be doing security reviews when deployments are frequent. In many organizations, security and compliance is a significant bottleneck for taking systems from "dev complete" to live. Involving infosec professionals throughout the development process also has the effect of improving communication and information flow—a win-win and a core goal of DevOps.

Compliance in the Federal Government

Federal information systems are subject to the Federal Information Security Management Act of 2002 (FISMA). FISMA requires that federal agencies follow NIST's Risk Management Framework (RMF). The RMF includes multiple steps, such as the preparation of a System Security Plan which documents how the relevant information security controls (325 for a moderate-impact system) have been implemented, and then an assessment resulting in a report (the security assessment report or SAR) which documents the validation of the implementation. This process can take from several months to over a year, and is often only *begun* once the system is "dev complete."

In order to reduce the time and cost taken to deliver federal information systems, a small team of civil servants at 18F created a platform as a service called cloud.gov based on an open-source version of Pivotal's Cloud Foundry, hosted on Amazon Web Services. Most of the controls in systems hosted on cloud.gov—269 of the 325 required for a moderate-impact information system—are taken care of at the platform level. Systems hosted on cloud.gov can go from dev complete to live in weeks, not months. This significantly reduces the amount of work—and thus cost—needed to implement the requirements of the Risk Management Framework.

Read more at https://18f.gsa.gov/2017/02/02/cloud-gov-is-now-fedramp-authorized/.

When building security into software is part of the daily work of developers, and when infosec teams provide tools, training, and support to make it easy for developers to do the right thing, delivery performance gets better. Furthermore, this has a positive impact on security. We found that high performers were spending 50% less time remediating security issues than low performers. In other words, by building security into their daily work, as opposed to retrofitting security concerns at the end, they spent significantly less time addressing security issues.

THE RUGGED MOVEMENT

Other names have been proposed to extend DevOps to cover infosec concerns. One is DevSecOps (coined by a few in the industry, including Topo Pal of Capital One and Shannon Lietz of Intuit). Another is Rugged DevOps, coined by Josh Corman and James Wickett. Rugged DevOps is the combination of DevOps with the *Rugged Manifesto*.

- I am rugged and, more importantly, my code is rugged.
- I recognize that software has become a foundation of our modern world.

- I recognize the awesome responsibility that comes with this foundational role.
- I recognize that my code will be used in ways I cannot anticipate, in ways it was not designed, and for longer than it was ever intended.
- I recognize that my code will be attacked by talented and persistent adversaries who threaten our physical, economic, and national security.
- I recognize these things—and I choose to be rugged.
- I am rugged because I refuse to be a source of vulnerability or weakness.
- I am rugged because I assure my code will support its mission.
- I am rugged because my code can face these challenges and persist in spite of them.
- I am rugged, not because it is easy, but because it is necessary and I am up for the challenge (Corman et al. 2012).

For the Rugged movement to succeed—and in line with DevOps principles—being rugged is everybody's responsibility.

CHAPTER 7

MANAGEMENT PRACTICES FOR SOFTWARE

The theory and practice of management in the context of software delivery has gone through significant change over the decades, with multiple paradigms in play. For many years, the project and program management paradigm, found in frameworks such as the Project Management Institute and PRINCE2, dominated. Following the release of the Agile Manifesto in 2001, Agile methods rapidly gained traction.

Meanwhile, ideas from the Lean movement in manufacturing began to be applied to software. This movement derives from Toyota's approach to manufacturing, originally designed to solve the problem of creating a wide variety of different types of cars for the relatively small Japanese market. Toyota's commitment to relentless improvement enabled the company to build cars faster, cheaper, and with higher quality than the competition. Companies such as Toyota and Honda cut deeply into the US auto manufacturing industry, which survived only by adopting their ideas and methods. The Lean philosophy was initially adapted for software development by Mary and Tom Poppendieck in their *Lean Software Development* book series.

In this chapter, we discuss management practices derived from the Lean movement and how they drive software delivery performance.

LEAN MANAGEMENT PRACTICES

In our research, we modeled Lean management and its application to software delivery with three components (Figure 7.1 along with lightweight change management, discussed later in this chapter):

1. Limiting work in progress (WIP), and using these limits to drive process improvement and increase throughput
2. Creating and maintaining visual displays showing key quality and productivity metrics and the current status of work (including defects), making these visual displays available to both engineers and leaders, and aligning these metrics with operational goals
3. Using data from application performance and infrastructure monitoring tools to make business decisions on a daily basis

Lean Management
Limit Work in Progress (WIP)
Visual Management
Feedback from Production
Lightweight Change Approvals

Figure 7.1: Components of Lean Management

The use of WIP limits and visual displays is well known in the Lean community. They are used to ensure that teams don't become overburdened (which may lead to longer lead times) and to expose obstacles to flow. What is most interesting is that WIP limits on their own do not strongly predict delivery performance. It's only when they're combined with the use of visual displays and have a feedback loop from production monitoring tools back to delivery teams or the business that we see a strong effect. When teams use these tools together, we see a much stronger positive effect on software delivery performance.

It is also worth going into a bit more detail on what exactly we're measuring. In the case of WIP, we're not just asking teams whether they are good at limiting their WIP and have processes in place to do so. We're also asking if their WIP limits make obstacles to higher flow visible, and if teams remove these obstacles through process improvement, leading to improved throughput. WIP limits are no good if they don't lead to improvements that increase flow.

In the case of visual displays, we ask if visual displays or dashboards are used to share information, and if teams use tools such as kanban or storyboards to organize their work. We also ask whether information on quality and productivity is readily available, if failures or defect rates are shown publicly using visual displays, and how readily this information is available. The central concepts here are the types of information being displayed, how broadly it is being shared, and how easy it is to access. Visibility, and the high-quality communication it enables, are key.

We hypothesized that in combination these practices increase delivery performance—and indeed they do. In fact, they also have positive effects on team culture and performance. As shown in Figure 7.2, these Lean management practices both decrease burnout (which we discuss in Chapter 9) and lead to a more generative culture (as described in Westrum's model in Chapter 3).

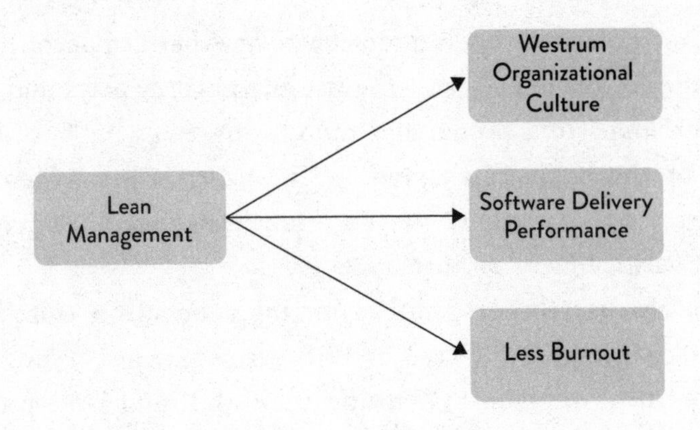

Figure 7.2: Impacts of Lean Management Practices

IMPLEMENT A LIGHTWEIGHT CHANGE MANAGEMENT PROCESS

Every organization will have some kind of process for making changes to their production environments. In a startup, this change management process may be something as simple as calling over another developer to review your code before pushing a change live. In large organizations, we often see change management processes that take days or weeks, requiring each change to be reviewed by a change advisory board (CAB) external to the team in addition to team-level reviews, such as a formal code review process.

We wanted to investigate the impact of change approval processes on software delivery performance. Thus, we asked about four possible scenarios:

1. All production changes must be approved by an external body (such as a manager or CAB).

2. Only high-risk changes, such as database changes, require approval.
3. We rely on peer review to manage changes.
4. We have no change approval process.

The results were surprising. We found that approval only for high-risk changes was not correlated with software delivery performance. Teams that reported no approval process or used peer review achieved higher software delivery performance. Finally, teams that required approval by an external body achieved lower performance.

We investigated further the case of approval by an external body to see if this practice correlated with stability. We found that external approvals were negatively correlated with lead time, deployment frequency, and restore time, and had no correlation with change fail rate. In short, approval by an external body (such as a manager or CAB) *simply doesn't work* to increase the stability of production systems, measured by the time to restore service and change fail rate. However, it certainly slows things down. It is, in fact, worse than having no change approval process at all.

Our recommendation based on these results is to use a lightweight change approval process based on peer review, such as pair programming or intrateam code review, combined with a deployment pipeline to detect and reject bad changes. This process can be used for all kinds of changes, including code, infrastructure, and database changes.

What About Segregation of Duties?

In regulated industries, segregation of duties is often required either explicitly in the wording of the regulation (for instance, in the case of PCI DSS) or by auditors. However, implementing this control does not require the use of a CAB or separate operations team. There are two mechanisms which can be effectively used to satisfy both the letter and the spirit of this control.

First, when any kind of change is committed, somebody who wasn't involved in authoring the change should review it either before or immediately following commit to version control. This can be somebody on the same team. This person should approve the change by recording their approval in a system of record such as GitHub (by approving the pull request) or a deployment pipeline tool (by approving a manual stage immediately following commit).

Second, changes should only be applied to production using a fully automated process that forms part of a deployment pipeline.[1] That is, no changes should be able to be made to production unless they have been committed to version control, validated by the standard build and test process, and then deployed through an automated process triggered through a deployment pipeline. As a result of implementing a deployment pipeline, auditors will have a complete record of which changes have been applied to which environments, where they come from in version control, what tests and validations have been run against them, and who approved them and when. A deployment pipeline is, thus, particularly valuable in the context of safety-critical or highly regulated industries.

Logically, it's clear why approval by external bodies is problematic. After all, software systems are complex. Every developer has made a seemingly innocuous change that took down part of the

---

[1] For more on deployment pipelines, see https://continuousdelivery.com/implementing/patterns/.

system. What are the chances that an external body, not intimately familiar with the internals of a system, can review tens of thousands of lines of code change by potentially hundreds of engineers and accurately determine the impact on a complex production system? This idea is a form of risk management theater: we check boxes so that when something goes wrong, we can say that at least we followed the process. At best, this process only introduces time delays and handoffs.

We think that there's a place for people outside teams to do effective risk management around changes. However, this is more of a governance role than actually inspecting changes. Such teams should be monitoring delivery performance and helping teams improve it by implementing practices that are known to increase stability, quality, and speed, such as the continuous delivery and Lean management practices described in this book.

CHAPTER 8

PRODUCT DEVELOPMENT

The Agile brand has more or less won the methodology wars. However, much of what has been implemented is *faux* Agile—people following some of the common practices while failing to address wider organizational culture and processes. For example, in larger companies it's still common to see months spent on budgeting, analysis, and requirements-gathering before work starts; to see work batched into big projects with infrequent releases; and for customer feedback to be treated as an afterthought. In contrast, both Lean product development and the Lean startup movement emphasize testing your product's design and business model by performing user research frequently, from the very beginning of the product lifecycle.

Eric Ries' book *The Lean Startup* (Ries 2011) created a surge of interest in lightweight approaches to exploring new business models and product ideas in conditions of uncertainty. Ries' work is a synthesis of ideas from the Lean movement, design thinking, and the work of entrepreneur Steve Blank (Blank 2013), which emphasizes the importance of taking an experimental approach to product development. This approach, based on our research, includes building and validating prototypes from the beginning, working in small batches, and evolving or "pivoting" products and the business models behind them early and often.

We wanted to test whether these practices have a direct impact on organizational performance, measured in terms of productivity, market share, and profitability.

LEAN PRODUCT DEVELOPMENT PRACTICES

We examined four capabilities which make up our model of a Lean approach to product development (see also Figure 8.1).

1. The extent to which teams slice up products and features into small batches that can be completed in less than a week and released frequently, including the use of MVPs (minimum viable products).
2. Whether teams have a good understanding of the flow of work from the business all the way through to customers, and whether they have visibility into this flow, including the status of products and features.
3. Whether organizations actively and regularly seek customer feedback and incorporate this feedback into the design of their products.
4. Whether development teams have the authority to create and change specifications as part of the development process without requiring approval.

Analysis showed that these factors were statistically significant in predicting higher software delivery performance and organizational performance, as well as improving organizational culture and decreasing burnout. By conducting our research over multiple years, we also found that software delivery performance predicts Lean product management practices. This reciprocal relationship,

Lean Product Development
Work in Small Batches
Make Flow of Work Visible
Gather & Implement Customer Feedback
Team Experimentation

Figure 8.1: Components of Lean Product Management

suggested by the literature, forms what is known as a virtuous cycle. Improving your software delivery effectiveness will improve your ability to work in small batches and incorporate customer feedback along the way.

Working in Small Batches

The key to working in small batches is to have work decomposed into features that allow for rapid development, instead of complex features developed on branches and released infrequently. This idea can be applied at both the feature and the product level. An MVP is a prototype of a product with just enough features to enable validated learning about the product and its business model. Working in small batches enables short lead times and faster feedback loops.

In software organizations, the capability to work and deliver in small batches is especially important because it allows you to gather user feedback quickly using techniques such as A/B testing. It's worth noting that an experimental approach to product development is highly correlated with the technical practices that contribute to continuous delivery.

Gathering customer feedback includes multiple practices: regularly collecting customer satisfaction metrics, actively seeking customer insights on the quality of products and features, and using this feedback to inform the design of products and features. The extent to which teams actually have the authority to respond to this feedback also turns out to be important.

TEAM EXPERIMENTATION

Many development teams working in organizations that claim to be Agile are nonetheless obliged to follow requirements created by different teams. This restriction can create some real problems and can result in products that don't actually delight and engage customers and won't deliver the expected business results.

One of the points of Agile development is to seek input from customers throughout the development process, including early stages. This allows the development team to gather important information, which then informs the next stages of development. But if a development team isn't allowed, without authorization from some outside body, to change requirements or specifications in response to what they discover, their ability to innovate is sharply inhibited.

Our analysis showed that the ability of teams to try out new ideas and create and update specifications during the development process, without requiring the approval of people outside the team, is an important factor in predicting organizational performance as measured in terms of profitability, productivity, and market share.

We're not proposing that you set your developers free to work on whatever ideas they like. To be effective, experimentation should be combined with the other capabilities we measure here: working in small batches, making the flow of work through the delivery process visible to everyone, and incorporating customer feedback into the design of products. This ensures that your teams are making well-reasoned, informed choices about the design, development, and delivery of work, and changing it based on feedback. This also ensures that the informed decisions they make are communicated throughout the organization. That increases the probability that the ideas and features they build will deliver delight to customers and add value to the organization.

EFFECTIVE PRODUCT MANAGEMENT DRIVES PERFORMANCE

We conducted our analysis of Lean product management capabilities over two years, from 2016–2017. In our first model, we saw that Lean product management practices positively impact software delivery performance, stimulate a generative culture, and decrease burnout.

In the following year, we flipped the model and confirmed that software delivery performance drives Lean product management practices. Improving your software delivery capability enables working in small batches and performing user research along the way, leading to better products. If we combine the models across years, it becomes a reciprocal model or, colloquially, a virtuous cycle. We also found that Lean product management practices predict organizational performance, measured in terms of productivity, profitability, and market share. The virtuous cycle of increased delivery performance and Lean product management practices drives better outcomes for your organization (see Figure 8.2).

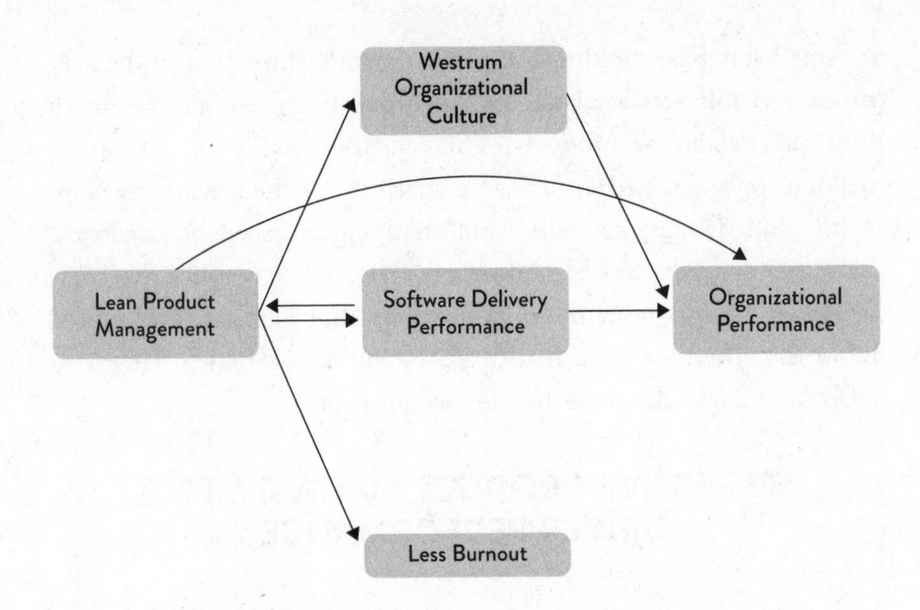

Figure 8.2: Impacts of Lean Product Management

In software organizations, the ability to work and deliver in small batches is especially important because it enables teams to integrate user research into product development and delivery. Furthermore, the ability to take an experimental approach to product development is highly correlated with the technical practices that contribute to continuous delivery.

CHAPTER 9

MAKING WORK SUSTAINABLE

To ensure that software delivery performance is not achieved through brute force or at the expense of the mental health of your team, our project investigated both burnout on teams and how painful the deployment process is. We measured these because we know they are important issues in the technology industry that contribute to illness, attrition, and millions of dollars of lost productivity.

DEPLOYMENT PAIN

The fear and anxiety that engineers and technical staff feel when they push code into production can tell us a lot about a team's software delivery performance. We call this deployment pain, and it is important to measure because it highlights the friction and disconnect that exist between the activities used to develop and test software and the work done to maintain and keep software operational. This is where development meets IT operations, and it is where there is the greatest potential for differences: in environment, in process and methodology, in mindset, and even in the words teams use to describe the work they do.

Our experience in the field and our interactions over the years with professionals building and deploying software kept highlighting the importance and salience of deployment pain. Because of this, we wanted to investigate deployment pain to see if it could be measured and, more importantly, if it was affected by DevOps practices. We found that where code deployments are most painful, you'll find the poorest software delivery performance, organizational performance, and culture.

The Benefits of Continuous Delivery at Microsoft

Microsoft engineering is one example of engineering teams feeling the benefits of continuous delivery. Thiago Almeida is a Senior Software Development Engineer Lead at Microsoft who drives cloud computing, open source, and DevOps practices on the Azure team. He spoke about the additional benefits of continuous delivery practices to his team, saying, "You may think that all of the benefits [are] going to your customers, but even inside of your company . . . [there are benefits]."[1] Before implementing the technical practices and discipline of continuous delivery on the Bing team, engineers reported work/life balance satisfaction scores of just 38%. After implementing these technical practices, the scores jumped to 75%. The difference is striking. It means the technical staff were better able to manage their professional duties during work hours, they didn't have to do deployment processes manually, and they were able to keep the stresses of work at work.

1 https://www.devopsdays.org/events/2016-london/program/thiago-almeida/.

While deployment pain can be an indication that software development and delivery is not sustainable in your organization, it is also a concern when development and test teams have no idea what deployments are like. If your teams have no visibility into code deployments—that is, if you ask your teams what software deployments are like and the answer is, "I don't know . . . I've never thought about it!"—that's another warning that software delivery performance could be low, because if developers or testers aren't aware of the deployment process, there are probably barriers hiding the work from them. And barriers that hide the work of deployment from developers are rarely good, because they isolate developers from the downstream consequences of their work.

We often have developers, and especially operations professionals, ask us, "What can be done to relieve deployment pain and improve the work of technical staff?" To answer this question, we included deployment pain in our research in 2015, 2016, and 2017. Based on our own experiences in software development and delivery and our time spent talking to people working with systems, we created a measure to capture how people feel when code is deployed. Measuring deployment pain ended up being relatively straightforward: we asked respondents if deployments were feared, disruptive in their work, or, in contrast, if they were easy and pain-free.

Our research shows that improving key technical capabilities reduces deployment pain: teams that implement comprehensive test and deployment automation; use continuous integration, including trunk-based development; shift left on security; effectively manage test data; use loosely coupled architectures; can work independently; and use version control of everything required to reproduce production environments decrease their deployment pain.

Put another way, the technical practices that improve our ability to deliver software with both speed and stability also reduce the stress and anxiety associated with pushing code to production. These technical practices are outlined in Chapters 4 and 5.

Statistical analysis also revealed a high correlation between deployment pain and key outcomes: the more painful code deployments are, the poorer the IT performance, organizational performance, and organizational culture.

How Painful Are Your Deployments?

If you want to know how your team is doing, just ask your team how painful deployments are and what specific things are causing that pain.

In particular, be aware that if deployments have to be performed outside of normal business hours, that's a sign of architectural problems that should be addressed. It's entirely possible—given sufficient investment—to build complex, large-scale distributed systems which allow for fully automated deployments with zero downtime.

Fundamentally, most deployment problems are caused by a complex, brittle deployment process. This is typically the result of three factors. First, software is often not written with deployability in mind. A common symptom here is when complex, orchestrated deployments are required because the software expects its environment and dependencies to be set up in a very particular way and does not tolerate any kind of deviation from these expectations, giving little useful information to administrators on what is wrong and why it is failing to operate correctly. (These characteristics also represent poor design for distributed systems.)

Second, the probability of a failed deployment rises substantially when manual changes must be made to production environments as part of the deployment process. Manual changes can easily lead to errors caused by typing, copy/paste mistakes, or poor or out-of-date documentation. Furthermore, environments whose configuration is managed manually often deviate substantially from each other (a problem known as "configuration drift"), leading to significant amounts of work at deploy time as operators debug to understand configuration differences, potentially making further manual changes that add to the problem.

Finally, complex deployments often require multiple handoffs between teams, particularly in siloed organizations where database administrators, network administrators, systems administrators, infosec, testing/QA, and developers all work in separate teams.

In order to reduce deployment pain, we should:

- Build systems that are designed to be deployed easily into multiple environments, can detect and tolerate failures in their environments, and can have various components of the system updated independently
- Ensure that the state of production systems can be reproduced (with the exception of production data) in an automated fashion from information in version control
- Build intelligence into the application and the platform so that the deployment process can be as simple as possible

Applications designed for a platform-as-a-service, such as Heroku, Pivotal Cloud Foundry, Red Hat OpenShift, Google Cloud Platform, Amazon Web Services, or Microsoft Azure, can typically be deployed using a single command.[2]

---

[2] One example of a set of architectural patterns that enable this kind of process can be found at https://12factor.net/.

Now that we've discussed deployment pain and covered some strategies to counteract it, let's move on to burnout. Deployment pain can lead to burnout if left unchecked.

BURNOUT

Burnout is physical, mental, or emotional exhaustion caused by overwork or stress—but it is more than just being overworked or stressed. Burnout can make the things we once loved about our work and life seem insignificant and dull. It often manifests itself as a feeling of helplessness, and is correlated with pathological cultures and unproductive, wasteful work.

The consequences of burnout are huge—for individuals and for their teams and organizations. Research shows that stressful jobs can be as bad for physical health as secondhand smoke (Goh et al. 2015) and obesity (Chandola et al. 2006). Symptoms of burnout include feeling exhausted, cynical, or ineffective; little or no sense of accomplishment in your work; and feelings about your work negatively affecting other aspects of your life. In extreme cases, burnout can lead to family issues, severe clinical depression, and even suicide.

Job stress also affects employers, costing the US economy $300 billion per year in sick time, long-term disability, and excessive job turnover (Maslach 2014). Thus, employers have both a duty of care toward employees and a fiduciary obligation to ensure staff do not become burned out.

Burnout can be prevented or reversed, and DevOps can help. Organizations can fix the conditions that lead to burnout by fostering a supportive work environment, by ensuring work is meaningful, and ensuring employees understand how their own work ties to strategic objectives.

As in other fast-paced, high-consequence work, software and technology is plagued by employee burnout. Technology managers, like so many other well-meaning managers, often try to fix the person while ignoring the work environment, even though changing the environment is far more vital for long-term success. Managers who want to avert employee burnout should concentrate their attention and efforts on:

- Fostering a respectful, supportive work environment that emphasizes learning from failures rather than blaming
- Communicating a strong sense of purpose
- Investing in employee development
- Asking employees what is preventing them from achieving their objectives and then fixing those things
- Giving employees time, space, and resources to experiment and learn

Last but not least, employees must be given the authority to make decisions that affect their work and their jobs, particularly in areas where they are responsible for the outcomes.

COMMON PROBLEMS THAT CAN LEAD TO BURNOUT

Christina Maslach, a professor of psychology at the University of California at Berkeley and a pioneering researcher on job burnout, found six organizational risk factors that predict burnout (Leiter and Maslach 2008):[3]

---

[3] We note that there are other models of burnout in the literature as well; one notable example is the work of Marie Åsberg, senior professor in the Department of Clinical Sciences at the Karolinska Institutet, Sweden. We focused on Maslach's work in our research.

1. Work overload: job demands exceed human limits.
2. Lack of control: inability to influence decisions that affect your job.
3. Insufficient rewards: insufficient financial, institutional, or social rewards.
4. Breakdown of community: unsupportive workplace environment.
5. Absence of fairness: lack of fairness in decision-making processes.
6. Value conflicts: mismatch in organizational values and the individual's values.

Maslach found that most organizations try to fix the person and ignore the work environment, even though her research shows that fixing the environment has a higher likelihood of success. All of the risk factors above are things that management and organizations have the power to change. We also refer the reader to Chapter 11 for more on the importance and impact of leadership and management in DevOps.

To measure burnout, we asked respondents:

- **If they felt burned out or exhausted.** Many of us know what burnout feels like, and we're often exhausted by it.
- **If they felt indifferent or cynical about their work, or if they felt ineffective.** A classic hallmark of burnout is indifference and cynicism, as well as feelings that your work is no longer helpful or effective.
- **If their work was having a negative effect on their life.** When your work starts negatively impacting your life outside of work, burnout has often set in.

Our research found that improving technical practices (such as those that contribute to continuous delivery) and Lean practices (such as those in Lean management and Lean product management) reduce feelings of burnout among our survey respondents.

HOW TO REDUCE OR FIGHT BURNOUT

Our own research tells us which organizational factors are most strongly correlated with high levels of burnout, and suggests where to look for solutions. The five most highly correlated factors are:

1. **Organizational culture.** Strong feelings of burnout are found in organizations with a pathological, power-oriented culture. Managers are ultimately responsible for fostering a supportive and respectful work environment, and they can do so by creating a blame-free environment, striving to learn from failures, and communicating a shared sense of purpose. Managers should also watch for other contributing factors and remember that human error is never the root cause of failure in systems.
2. **Deployment pain.** Complex, painful deployments that must be performed outside of business hours contribute to high stress and feelings of lack of control.[4] With the right practices in place, deployments don't have to be painful events. Managers and leaders should ask their teams how painful their deployments are and fix the things that hurt the most.

[4] Note that postdeployment pain is also important to watch for. Broken systems that are constantly paging your on-call staff after hours are disruptive and unhealthy.

3. **Effectiveness of leaders.** Responsibilities of a team leader include limiting work in process and eliminating roadblocks for the team so they can get their work done. It's not surprising that respondents with effective team leaders reported lower levels of burnout.
4. **Organizational investments in DevOps.** Organizations that invest in developing the skills and capabilities of their teams get better outcomes. Investing in training and providing people with the necessary support and resources (including time) to acquire new skills are critical to the successful adoption of DevOps.
5. **Organizational performance.** Our data shows that Lean management and continuous delivery practices help improve software delivery performance, which in turn improves organizational performance. At the heart of Lean management is giving employees the necessary time and resources to improve their own work. This means creating a work environment that supports experimentation, failure, and learning, and allows employees to make decisions that affect their jobs. This also means creating space for employees to do new, creative, value-add work *during the work week*—and not just expecting them to devote extra time after hours. A good example of this is Google's 20% time policy, where the company allows employees 20% of their week to work on new projects, or IBM's "THINK Friday" program, where Friday afternoons are designated for time without meetings and employees are encouraged to work on new and exciting projects they normally don't have time for.

A point worth mentioning is the importance of values alignment and its role in fighting burnout. When organizational values and individual values aren't aligned, you are more likely to see burnout in employees, particularly in demanding and high-risk work like technology. We have seen this all too often, and the effects are unfortunate and widespread.

We think the opposite is more promising and actionable: when organizational values and individual values are aligned, the effects of burnout can be lessened and even counteracted. For example, if an individual strongly values environmental causes, but the organization dumps waste into nearby rivers and spends money to lobby their government representatives to allow this to continue, there will be a lack of alignment. This individual will likely be much happier working for an organization with a strong commitment to corporate social responsibility in green initiatives. This is an area of potential impact that organizations neglect at their own peril. By aligning organizational values with individual values, employee burnout can be reduced. Imagine the effects on employee satisfaction, productivity, and retention. The potential value to organizations and the economy is staggering.

It is important to note that the organizational values we mention here are the real, actual, lived organizational values felt by employees. If the organizational values felt by employees differ from the official values of the organization—the mission statements printed on pieces of paper or even on placards—it will be the everyday, lived values that count. If there is a values mismatch—either between an employee and their organization, or between the organization's stated values and their actual values—burnout will be a concern. When there is alignment, employees will thrive.

In summary, our research found evidence that technical and Lean management practices contributed to reductions in both burnout and deployment pain. This is summarized in Figure 9.1. These findings have serious implications for technology organizations: not only do investments in technology make our software development and delivery better, they make the work lives of our professionals better.

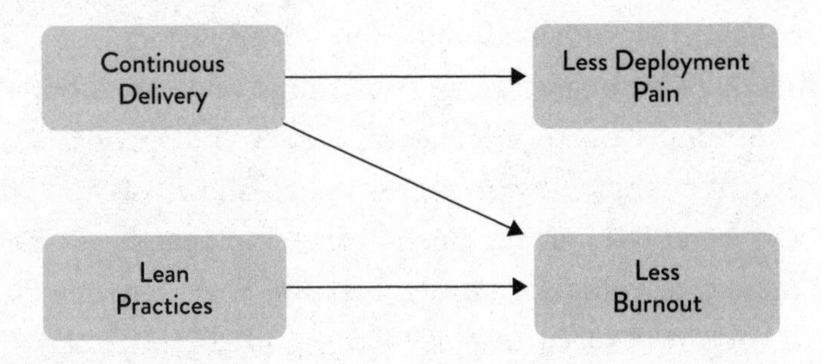

Figure 9.1: Impacts of Technical and Lean Practices on Work Life

We have discussed the important components of organizational culture and ways to both improve and measure it. We will now turn to details of identity and employee satisfaction—and what it means for technology transformations.

CHAPTER 10

EMPLOYEE SATISFACTION, IDENTITY, AND ENGAGEMENT

People are at the heart of every technology transformation. With market pressures to deliver technology and solutions ever faster, the importance of hiring, retaining, and engaging our workforce is greater than ever. Every good manager knows this, but there is still a lack of information on how to measure these outcomes and on what impacts them, particularly in the context of technology transformations.

We wanted to include in our study the people affected by DevOps adoptions—to see what could improve their work and if these improvements had impacts on the organization. Our research found that employee engagement and satisfaction are indicative of employee loyalty and identity, can help reduce burnout, and can drive key organizational outcomes like profitability, productivity, and market share. We also show you how to measure these key employee factors so you can implement them in your own teams—whether you're a leader, manager, or an interested practitioner.

In this chapter, we discuss employee loyalty (as measured by employee Net Promoter Score and identity) and job satisfaction, and then close with a discussion of diversity.

EMPLOYEE LOYALTY

To understand employee engagement in the context of technology transformations and DevOps, we looked at it through the lens of a broadly used benchmark of customer loyalty: Net Promoter Score (NPS).

High performers have better employee loyalty, as measured by employee Net Promoter Score (eNPS). Our research found that employees in high-performing organizations were 2.2 times more likely to recommend their organization as a great place to work, and other studies have also shown that this is correlated with better business outcomes (Azzarello et al. 2012).

MEASURING NPS

Net Promoter Score is calculated based on a single question: How likely is it that you would recommend our company/product/service to a friend or colleague?

Net Promoter Score is scored on a 0–10 scale, and is categorized as follows:

- Customers who give a score of 9 or 10 are considered promoters. Promoters create greater value for the company because they tend to buy more, cost less to acquire and retain, stay longer, and generate positive word of mouth.
- Those giving a score of 7 or 8 are passives. Passives are satisfied, but much less enthusiastic customers. They are less likely to provide referrals and more likely to defect if something better comes along.

- Those giving a score from 0 to 6 are detractors. Detractors are more expensive to acquire and retain, they defect faster, and can hurt the business through negative word of mouth.

In our study, we asked two questions to capture the employee Net Promoter Score:

1. Would you recommend your ORGANIZATION as a place to work to a friend or colleague?
2. Would you recommend your TEAM as a place to work to a friend or colleague?

We compared the proportion of promoters (those who scored 9 or 10) in the high-performing group against those in the low-performing group. We found that employees in high-performing teams were 2.2 times more likely to recommend their *organization* to a friend as a great place to work, and 1.8 times more likely to recommend their *team* to a friend.

This is a significant finding, as research has shown that "companies with highly engaged workers grew revenues two and a half times as much as those with low engagement levels. And [publicly traded] stocks of companies with a high-trust work environment outperformed market indexes by a factor of three from 1997 through 2011" (Azzarello et al. 2012).

Employee engagement is not just a feel-good metric—it drives business outcomes. We found that the employee Net Promoter Score was significantly correlated with the following constructs:

- The extent to which the organization collects customer feedback and uses it to inform the design of products and features

- The ability of teams to visualize and understand the flow of products or features through development all the way to the customer
- The extent to which employees identify with their organization's values and goals, and the effort they are willing to put in to make the organization successful

As we demonstrated in Chapter 8, when employees see the connection between the work they do and its positive impact on customers, they identify more strongly with the company's purpose, which leads to better software delivery and organizational performance.

NPS Explained

While this may seem like a simplistic measure, research has shown that NPS correlates to company growth in many industries (Reichheld 2003). Similar to company NPS, employee Net Promoter Score (eNPS) is used to measure employee loyalty.

There's a link between employees' loyalty and their work: loyal employees are the most engaged and do their best work, often going the extra mile to deliver better customer experiences—which in turn drives company performance.

NPS is calculated by subtracting the percentage of detractors from the percentage of promoters. For example, if 40% of employees are detractors and only 20% are promoters, the Net Promoter Score is –20%.

CHANGING ORGANIZATIONAL CULTURE AND IDENTITY

People are an organization's greatest asset—yet so often they're treated like expendable resources. When leaders invest in their people and enable them to do their best work, employees identify more strongly with the organization and are willing to go the extra mile to help it be successful. In return, organizations get higher levels of performance and productivity, which lead to better outcomes for the business. These findings are shown in Figure 10.1.

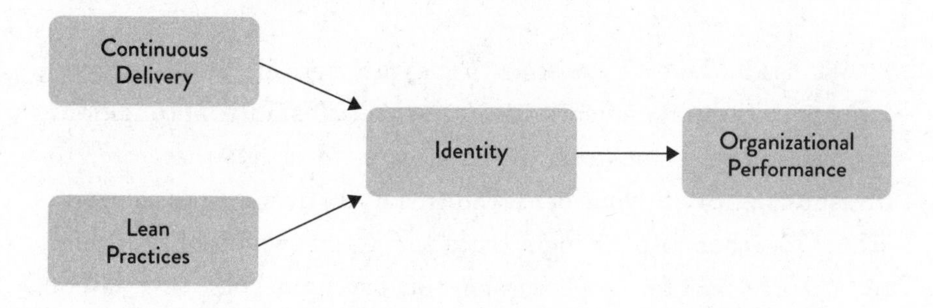

Figure 10.1: Impacts of Technical and Lean Practices on Identity

Effective management practices combined with technical approaches, such as continuous delivery, don't just impact performance, they also have a measurable effect on organizational culture. As we continued our research, we added a new measure: the extent to which survey respondents identify with the organizations they work for. To measure this, we asked people the extent to which they agreed with the following statements (adapted from Kankanhalli et al. 2005):

- I am glad I chose to work for this organization rather than another company.
- I talk of this organization to my friends as a great company to work for.
- I am willing to put in a great deal of effort beyond what is normally expected to help my organization be successful.
- I find that my values and my organization's values are very similar.
- In general, the people employed by my organization are working toward the same goal.
- I feel that my organization cares about me.

We used a Likert-type scale to measure agreement or disagreement with these statements. The items met all statistical conditions for measuring a construct (in this case, *identity*); therefore, to measure identity in your own teams, you can average the five item scores together into a single score for a person's identity. (Refer to Chapter 13 for a discussion of psychometrics and latent constructs.)

Our key hypothesis in asking these questions was that teams implementing continuous delivery practices and taking an experimental approach to product development will build better products, and will also feel more connected to the rest of their organization. This, in turn, creates a virtuous cycle: by creating higher levels of software delivery performance, we increase the rate at which teams can validate their ideas, creating higher levels of job satisfaction and organizational performance.

Another key point is that identity includes values alignment with the goals of the team and organization. Recall from the previous chapter that one of the key contributors to burnout is a mismatch of personal and organizational values. What this tells us is that a sense of identity can help reduce burnout by aligning personal and organizational values. Therefore, investments in continuous delivery and Lean management practices, which contribute to a stronger sense of identity, may very well help reduce burnout. Once again, this creates a virtuous circle of value creation in the business where investments in technology and process that make the work better for our people are essential for delivering value for our customers and the business.

This is in contrast to the way many companies still work: requirements are handed down to development teams who must then deliver large stacks of work in batches. In this model, employees feel little control over the products they build and the customer outcomes they create, and little connection to the organizations they work for. This is immensely demotivating for teams and leads to employees feeling emotionally disconnected from their work—and to worse organizational outcomes.

The extent to which people identified with their organization predicted a generative, performance-oriented culture and also predicted organizational performance, as measured in terms of productivity, market share, and profitability. That shouldn't surprise us. If people are a company's greatest asset—and many corporate leaders declare they are—then having employees who strongly identify with the company should prove a competitive advantage.

Adrian Cockcroft, Netflix's seminal cloud architect, was once asked by a senior leader in a Fortune 500 company where he got his amazing people from. Cockcroft replied, "I hired them from you!" (personal communication). Our analysis is clear: in today's fast-moving and competitive world, the best thing you can do for your products, your company, and your people is institute a culture of experimentation and learning, and invest in the technical and management capabilities that enable it. As Chapter 3 shows, a healthy organizational culture contributes to hiring and retention, and the best, most innovative companies are capitalizing on this.

HOW DOES JOB SATISFACTION IMPACT ORGANIZATIONAL PERFORMANCE?

We mentioned the virtuous circle earlier in reference to software delivery performance, and we see it at work here, too: people who feel supported by their employers, who have the tools and resources to do their work, and who feel their judgment is valued, turn out better work. Better work results in higher software delivery performance, which results in a higher level of organizational performance. We show these findings in Figure 10.2.

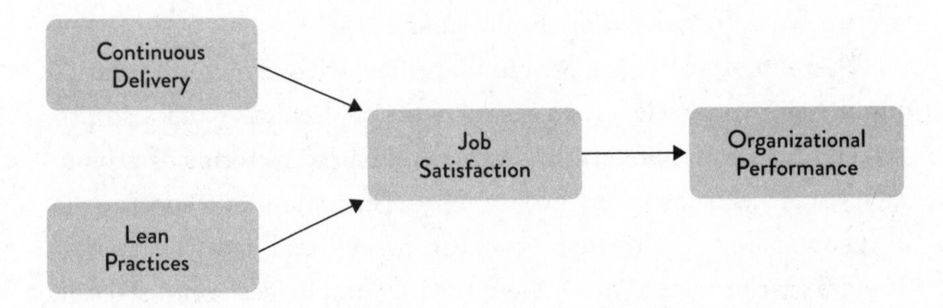

Figure 10.2: Impacts of Technical and Lean Practices on Job Satisfaction

This cycle of continuous improvement and learning is what sets successful companies apart, enabling them to innovate, get ahead of the competition—and win.

HOW DOES DEVOPS CONTRIBUTE TO JOB SATISFACTION?

Although DevOps is first and foremost about culture, it's important to note that job satisfaction depends strongly on having the right tools and resources to do your work. In fact, our measure of job satisfaction looks at a few key things: if you are satisfied in your work, if you are given the tools and resources to do your work, and if your job makes good use of your skills and abilities. It's important to call these out, because taken together, this is what makes job satisfaction so impactful.

Tools are an important component of DevOps practices, and many of these tools enable automation. Furthermore, we found that good DevOps technical practices predict job satisfaction. Automation matters because it gives over to computers the things computers are good at—rote tasks that require no thinking and that in fact are done better when you don't think too much about them. Since humans are so bad at these kinds of tasks, turning them over to computers allows people to focus on the things they're good at: weighing the evidence, thinking through problems, and making decisions. Being able to apply one's judgment and experience to challenging problems is a big part of what makes people satisfied with their work.

Looking at the measures that correlate strongly with job satisfaction, we see some commonalities. Practices like proactive monitoring and test and deployment automation all automate menial tasks and require people to make decisions based on a feedback loop. Instead of managing tasks, people get to make decisions, employing their skills, experience, and judgment.

DIVERSITY IN TECH—WHAT OUR RESEARCH FOUND

Diversity matters. Research shows that teams with more diversity with regard to gender or underrepresented minorities are smarter (Rock and Grant 2016), achieve better team performance (Deloitte 2013), and achieve better business outcomes (Hunt et al. 2015). Our research shows that few teams are diverse in this regard. We recommend that teams wanting to achieve high performance do their best to recruit and retain more women and underrepresented minorities, and work to improve diversity in other areas too, such as people with disabilities.

It is also important to note that diversity is not enough. Teams and organizations must also be inclusive. An inclusive organization is one where "*all* organizational members feel welcome and valued for who they are and what they 'bring to the table.' All stakeholders share a high sense of belonging and fulfilled mutual purpose" (Smith and Lindsay 2014, p. 1). Inclusion must be present in order for diversity to take hold.

WOMEN IN DEVOPS

We started asking questions about gender in 2015, which sparked some lively discussion in social media on the topic of women in tech. We heard everything from wholehearted support from many women and men in the DevOps community to questions about why gender diversity in tech matters. Of the total respondents, 5% self-identified as female in 2015, 6% in 2016, and 6.5% in 2017. These numbers were much lower than we expected, given that women made up about 7% in 2011 (SAGE 2012), down from 13% in 2008 (SAGE 2008) in systems administration and 27% in computer and information management (Diaz and King 2013). We were hoping to find more reassuring numbers of women working on technical teams.

Figure 10.3: Gender Demographics in 2017 Study

Among survey respondents:

- 33% reported working on teams with no women.
- 56% reported working on teams that were less than 10% female.
- 81% reported working on teams that were less than 25% female.

We started our research around binary gender because that allowed us to compare our results with existing research. We hope to extend our work into non-binary gender in the future. We can report basic statistics about reported gender for the 2017 study (see also Figure 10.3):

- 91% Male
- 6% Female
- 3% Non-binary or other

UNDERREPRESENTED MINORITIES IN DEVOPS

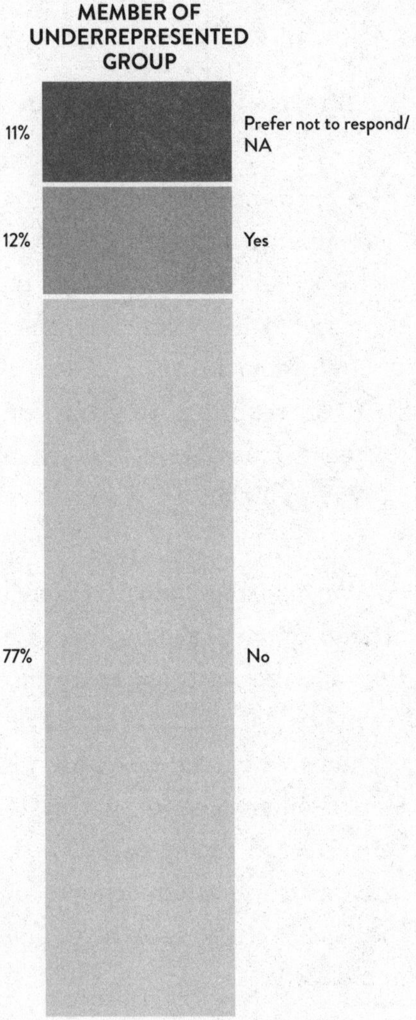

MEMBER OF UNDERREPRESENTED GROUP

11% Prefer not to respond/ NA

12% Yes

77% No

Figure 10.4: Underrepresented Minority Demographics in 2017 Study

We also asked if respondents identified as an underrepresented minority (see also Figure 10.4).

- 77% responded no, I do not identify as underrepresented.
- 12% responded yes, I identify as underrepresented.
- 11% responded that they preferred not to respond or NA.

Because the data was collected around the world, this self-identification was as specific as we could get. For example, the United States identifies and defines several ethnicities and nationalities as minority groups (e.g., African American, Hispanic, Pacific Islander, etc.) that do not exist or would not make sense as identifiers in other countries around the world.

We have not extended our research into people with disabilities yet, but hope to in the future.

WHAT OTHER RESEARCH TELLS US ABOUT DIVERSITY

Most research in diversity looks at binary gender, so let's start there. What does the current research tell us? There's plenty of research linking the presence of women in leadership positions to higher financial performance (McGregor 2014), stock market performance (Covert July 2014), and hedge fund returns (Covert January 2014). Furthermore, a study conducted by Anita Woolley and Thomas W. Malone measured group intelligence and found that teams with more women tended to fall above average on the collective intelligence scale (Woolley and Malone 2011). Despite all of these clear advantages, organizations are failing to recruit and retain women in technical fields.

Since there are no significant differences between men and women in terms of ability or aptitude in STEM (science, technology, engineering, and mathematics) fields (Leslie et al. 2015), what's keeping women and other underrepresented groups out of tech?[1] The answer could be nothing more than the pervasive belief that some men are naturally more suited to technical work because they possess innate brilliance (Leslie et al. 2015).

It is that pervasive belief that seeps into our culture, creating an environment in which it is increasingly difficult for women to stay (Snyder 2014). Women are leaving tech at a 45% higher rate than men (Quora 2017), and the outlook for minorities is likely similar. Women and underrepresented minorities report harassment, microaggressions, and unequal pay (e.g., Mundy 2017). These are all things we can actively watch for and improve as leaders and peers.

---

[1] Note that Leslie et al.'s study only investigated women and African Americans, but the findings are likely generalizable to other underrepresented minorities.

WHAT WE CAN DO

It's up to all of us to prioritize diversity and promote inclusive environments. It's good for your team and it's good for the business. Here are some resources to help you get started:

- Anita Borg Institute has excellent tools for advancing women in technology. It includes the Grace Hopper Conference. Though not without its issues, it's an empowering experience for many women to be able to attend an all- or largely-women technical conference, pulling over 18,000 women in 2017 alone.[2]
- Geek Feminism is a great online resource for supporting women in geek communities.[3]
- Project Include is a fantastic resource to support diversity along several axes, all online and open source.[4]

---

2 https://anitab.org/.

3 http://geekfeminism.wikia.com/wiki/Geek_Feminism_Wiki.

4 http://projectinclude.org/.

CHAPTER 11

LEADERS AND MANAGERS

Over the years, our research has investigated the effects of various technical and Lean management practices on software delivery performance as well as team culture. However, in the early years of the project, we hadn't directly studied the effects of leadership on DevOps practices.

This chapter will present our findings on the role of leaders and managers in technology transformations, as well as outline some steps that leaders can take to improve the culture in their own teams.

TRANSFORMATIONAL LEADERSHIP

Not sure of how important technology leadership is? Consider this: by 2020, half of the CIOs who have not transformed their teams' capabilities will be displaced from their organizations' digital leadership teams (Gartner).

That's because leadership really does have a powerful impact on results. Being a leader doesn't mean you have people reporting to you on an organizational chart—leadership is about inspiring and motivating those around you. A good leader affects a team's ability to deliver code, architect good systems, and apply Lean principles to how the team manages its work and develops products. All of these have a measurable impact on an organization's profitability, productivity, and market share. These also have an impact on customer satisfaction, efficiency, and the ability to achieve organizational goals—noncommercial goals that are important for profit-seeking and not-for-profit organizations alike. However, these effects on organizational and noncommercial goals are all indirect, through the technical and Lean practices that leaders support in their teams.

In our opinion, the role of leadership on technology transformation has been one of the more overlooked topics in DevOps, despite the fact that transformational leadership is essential for:

- Establishing and supporting generative and high-trust cultural norms
- Creating technologies that enable developer productivity, reducing code deployment lead times and supporting more reliable infrastructures
- Supporting team experimentation and innovation, and creating and implementing better products faster
- Working across organizational silos to achieve strategic alignment

Unfortunately, within the DevOps community we have sometimes been guilty of maligning leadership—for example, when middle managers or conservative holdouts prevent teams from making changes needed to improve software delivery and organizational performance.

And yet, one of the most common questions we hear is, "How do we get leaders on board, so we can make the necessary changes?" We all recognize that engaged leadership is essential for successful DevOps transformations. Leaders have the authority and budget to make the large-scale changes that are often needed, to provide air cover when a transformation is underway, and to change the incentives of entire groups of technical professionals—whether they are in development, QA, operations, or information security. Leaders are those who set the tone of the organization and reinforce the desired cultural norms.

To capture transformational leadership, we used a model that includes five dimensions (Rafferty and Griffin 2004). According to this model, the five characteristics of a transformational leader are:

- **Vision.** Has a clear understanding of where the organization is going and where it should be in five years.
- **Inspirational communication.** Communicates in a way that inspires and motivates, even in an uncertain or changing environment.
- **Intellectual stimulation.** Challenges followers to think about problems in new ways.
- **Supportive leadership.** Demonstrates care and consideration of followers' personal needs and feelings.
- **Personal recognition.** Praises and acknowledges achievement of goals and improvements in work quality; personally compliments others when they do outstanding work.

What Is Transformational Leadership?

Transformational leadership means leaders inspiring and motivating followers to achieve higher performance by appealing to their values and sense of purpose, facilitating wide-scale organizational change. Such leaders encourage their teams to work toward a common goal through their vision, values, communication, example-setting, and their evident caring about their followers' personal needs.

It has been observed that there are similarities between servant leadership and transformational leadership, but they differ in the leader's focus. Servant leaders focus on their followers' development and performance, whereas transformational leaders focus on getting followers to identify with the organization and engage in support of organizational objectives.

We also selected transformational leadership as the model to use in our research because it is more predictive of performance outcomes in other contexts, and we were interested in understanding how to improve performance in technology.

We measured transformational leadership using survey questions adapted from Rafferty and Griffin (2004):[1]

My leader or manager:

- (Vision)
  - Has a clear understanding of where we are going.
  - Has a clear sense of where he/she wants our team to be in five years.
  - Has a clear idea of where the organization is going.
- (Inspirational communication)
  - Says things that make employees proud to be a part of this organization.
  - Says positive things about the work unit.

[1] Our analysis confirmed these questions were good measures of transformational leadership. See Chapter 13 for a discussion of latent constructs and Appendix C for the statistical methods used.

- Encourages people to see changing environments as situations full of opportunities.

- (Intellectual stimulation)
  - Challenges me to think about old problems in new ways.
  - Has ideas that have forced me to rethink some things that I have never questioned before.
  - Has challenged me to rethink some of my basic assumptions about my work.
- (Supportive leadership)
  - Considers my personal feelings before acting.
  - Behaves in a manner which is thoughtful of my personal needs.
  - Sees that the interests of employees are given due consideration.
- (Personal recognition)
  - Commends me when I do a better than average job.
  - Acknowledges improvement in my quality of work.
  - Personally compliments me when I do outstanding work.

Our analysis found that these characteristics of transformational leadership are highly correlated with software delivery performance. In fact, we observed significant differences in leadership characteristics among high-, medium-, and low-performing teams. High-performing teams reported having leaders with the strongest behaviors across all dimensions: vision, inspirational communication, intellectual stimulation, supportive leadership, and personal recognition. In contrast, low-performing teams reported the lowest levels of these leadership characteristics. These differences were all at statistically significant levels. When we take our analysis one step further, we find that teams with the least transformative leaders are far less likely to be high performers. Specifically, teams that report leadership in the bottom one-third of leadership strength are only half as likely to be high performers. This validates our common experience: though we often hear stories of DevOps and technology transformation success coming from the grassroots, it is far easier to achieve success when you have leadership support.

We also found that transformational leadership is highly correlated with employee Net Promoter Score. We find transformational leaders in places where employees are happy, loyal, and engaged. Although our research didn't include measures of transformational leadership and organizational culture in the same year, other studies have found that strong transformational leaders build and support healthy team and organizational cultures (Rafferty and Griffin 2004).

A transformational leader's influence is seen through their support of their teams' work, be that in technical practices or product management capabilities. The positive (or negative) influence of leadership flows all the way through to software delivery performance and organizational performance. We show this in Figure 11.1.

Said another way, we found evidence that leaders alone cannot achieve high DevOps outcomes. We looked at the performance of teams with the strongest transformational leaders—those with the top 10% of reported transformational leadership characteristics. One might think that these teams would have better than average performance. However, these teams were equally or even less likely to be high performers compared to the entire population of teams represented in survey results.

This makes sense, because *leaders cannot achieve goals on their own*. They need their teams executing the work on a suitable architecture, with good technical practices, use of Lean principles, and all the other factors that we've studied over the years.

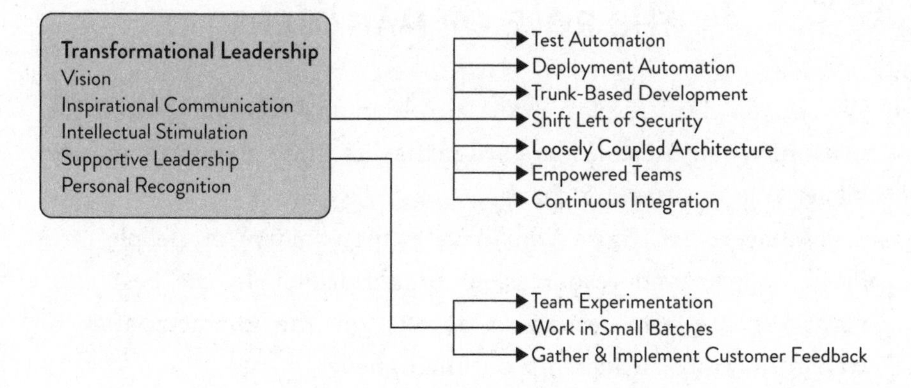

Figure 11.1: Impacts of Transformational Leadership on Technical and Lean Capabilities

In summary, we found that leadership helps build great teams, great technology, and great organizations—but indirectly, leadership enables teams to rearchitect their systems and implement the necessary continuous delivery and Lean management practices.

Transformational leadership enables the practices that correlate with high performance, and it also supports effective communication and collaboration between team members in pursuit of organizational goals. Such leadership also provides the foundation for a culture in which continuous experimentation and learning is part of everybody's daily work.

The behavior of transformational leaders thus enhances and enables the values, processes, and practices that our research has identified. It is not a separate behavior or a new set of practices—it just amplifies the effectiveness of the technical and organizational practices we have been studying over several years.

THE ROLE OF MANAGERS

We see that leaders play a critical role in any technology transformation. When those leaders are managers, they may have an even bigger role in affecting change.

Managers are those who have responsibility for people, and often budgets and resources, in organizations. In the best case, managers are also leaders and take on the characteristics of transformational leadership outlined above.

Managers, in particular, play a critical role in connecting the strategic objectives of the business to the work their teams do. Managers can do a lot to improve their team's performance by creating a work environment where employees feel safe, investing in developing the capabilities of their people, and removing obstacles to work.

We also found that investment in DevOps is highly correlated with software delivery performance. When it comes to culture, managers can improve matters by enabling specific DevOps practices in their teams and by visibly investing in DevOps and in their employees' professional development.

Managers can also facilitate big improvements in software delivery performance by taking measures to make deployments less painful. Last but not least, managers should make performance metrics visible and take pains to align these with organizational goals, and should delegate more authority to their employees. Knowledge is power, and you should give power to those who have the knowledge.

You may be asking yourself: What could investment in DevOps initiatives and my teams look like? There are a number of ways technology leaders can invest in their teams:

- Ensure that existing resources are made available and accessible to everyone in the organization. Create space and opportunities for learning and improving.
- Establish a dedicated training budget and make sure people know about it. Also, give your staff the latitude to choose training that interests them. This training budget may include dedicated time during the day to make use of resources that already exist in the organization.
- Encourage staff to attend technical conferences at least once a year and summarize what they learned for the entire team.
- Set up internal hack days, where cross-functional teams can get together to work on a project.
- Encourage teams to organize internal "yak days," where teams get together to work on technical debt. These are great events because technical debt is so rarely prioritized.
- Hold regular internal DevOps mini-conferences. We've seen organizations achieve success using the classic DevOpsDays format, which combines pre-prepared talks with "open spaces" where participants self-organize to propose and facilitate their own sessions.
- Give staff dedicated time, such as 20% time or several days after a release, to experiment with new tools and technologies. Allocate budget and infrastructure for special projects.

TIPS TO IMPROVE CULTURE AND SUPPORT YOUR TEAMS

As the real value of a leader or manager is manifest in how they amplify the work of their teams, perhaps the most valuable work they can do is growing and supporting a strong organizational culture among those they serve: their teams. This allows the experts that work with and for them to operate at maximum effectiveness, creating value for the organization.

In this section, we list some easy ways managers, team leads, and even engaged practitioners can support the culture in their teams. Our research shows that three things are highly correlated with software delivery performance and contribute to a strong team culture: cross-functional collaboration, a climate for learning, and tools.

Enable cross-functional collaboration by:

- **Building trust with your counterparts on other teams.** Building trust between teams is the most important thing you can do, and it must be built over time. Trust is built on kept promises, open communication, and behaving predictably even in stressful situations. Your teams will be able to work more effectively, and the relationship will signal to the organization that cross-functional collaboration is valued.
- **Encouraging practitioners to move between departments.** An admin or engineer may find as they build their skills that they're interested in a role in a different department. This sort of lateral move can be incredibly valuable to both teams. Practitioners bring valuable information about processes and challenges to their new team, and members of the previous team have a natural point person when reaching out to collaborate.
- **Actively seeking, encouraging, and rewarding work that facilitates collaboration.** Make sure success is reproducible and pay attention to latent factors that make collaboration easier.

Use Disaster Recovery Testing Exercises to Build Relationships

Many large technology companies run disaster recovery testing exercises, or "game days," in which outages are simulated or actually created according to a pre-prepared plan, and teams must work together to maintain or restore service levels.

Kripa Krishnan, Director of Cloud Operations at Google, runs a team that plans and executes these exercises. She reports, "For DiRT-style events to be successful, an organization first needs to accept system and process failures as a means of learning . . . We design tests that require engineers from several groups who might not normally work together to interact with each other. That way, should a real large-scale disaster ever strike, these people will already have strong working relationships" (ACMQueue 2012).

Help create a climate of learning by:

- **Creating a training budget and advocating for it internally.** Emphasize how much the organization values a climate of learning by putting resources behind formal education opportunities.
- **Ensuring that your team has the resources to engage in informal learning and the space to explore ideas.** Learning often happens outside of formal education. Some companies, like 3M and Google, have famously set aside a portion of time (15% and 20%, respectively) for focused free-thinking and exploration of side projects.

- **Making it safe to fail.** If failure is punished, people won't try new things. Treating failures as opportunities to learn and holding blameless postmortems to work out how to improve processes and systems helps people feel comfortable taking (reasonable) risks, and helps create a culture of innovation.
- **Creating opportunities and spaces to share information.** Whether you create weekly lightning talks or offer resources for monthly lunch-and-learns, set up a regular cadence of opportunities for employees to share their knowledge.
- **Encourage sharing and innovation by having demo days and forums.** This allows teams to share what they have created with each other. This also lets the teams celebrate their work and learn from each other.

Make effective use of tools:

- **Make sure your team can choose their tools.** Unless there's a good reason not to, practitioners should choose their own tools. If they can build infrastructure and applications the way they want, they're much more likely to be invested in their work. This is backed up in the data: one of the major contributors to job satisfaction is whether employees feel they have the tools and resources to do their job (see Chapter 10). We also see this in our data as one of the predictors of continuous delivery: teams that are empowered to choose their own tools drive software delivery performance (see Chapter 5). If your organization must standardize tools, ensure that procurement and finance are acting in the interests of teams, not the other way around.

- **Make monitoring a priority.** Refine your infrastructure and application monitoring system, and make sure you're collecting information on the right services and putting that information to good use. The visibility and transparency yielded by effective monitoring are invaluable. Proactive monitoring was strongly related to performance and job satisfaction in our survey, and it is a key part of a strong technical foundation (see Chapters 7 and 10).

While many DevOps success stories highlight the fantastic grassroots efforts of the technical teams involved, our experience and our research shows that technology transformations benefit from truly engaged and transformational leaders who can support and amplify the work of their teams. This support carries through to deliver value to the business, so organizations would be wise to see leadership development as an investment in their teams, their technology, and their products.

PART TWO
THE RESEARCH

To establish what we presented in Part I, we had to go beyond case studies and stories and into rigorous research methods. This allowed us to identify the practices that are the strongest predictors of success for all organizations of any size in any industry.

In the first part of the book, we discussed the results of this research program and outlined why technology is a key value driver and differentiator for all organizations today. Now, we present the science behind the research findings in Part I.

CHAPTER 12

THE SCIENCE BEHIND THIS BOOK

Every day, our news feeds are full of strategies designed to make our lives easier, make us happier, and help us take over the world. We also hear stories about how teams and organizations use different strategies to transform their technology and win in the market. But how are we to know which actions we take just *happen* to correspond to the changes we observe in our environment and which actions are driving these changes? This is where rigorous primary research comes into play. But what do we mean by "rigorous" and "primary"?

PRIMARY AND SECONDARY RESEARCH

Research falls into two broad classes: primary and secondary research. The key difference between these two types is who collects the data. Secondary research utilizes data that was collected by someone else. Examples of secondary research you are probably familiar with are book reports or research reports we all completed in school or university: we collected existing information, summarized it, and (hopefully) added in our own insights about what was found. Common examples of this also include case studies and some market research reports. Secondary research reports can be valuable, particularly if the existing data is difficult to find, the summary is particularly insightful, or the reports are delivered at regular intervals. Secondary research is generally faster and less expensive to conduct, but the data may not be well suited to the research team because they are bound by whatever data already exists.

In contrast, primary research involves collecting new data by the research team. An example of primary research includes the United States Census. The research team collects new data every ten years to report on demographic and population statistics for the country. Primary research is valuable because it can report information that is not already known and provide insights that are not available in existing datasets. Primary research gives researchers more power and control over the questions they can address, though it is generally more costly and time intensive to conduct. This book and the State of DevOps Reports are based on primary research.

QUALITATIVE AND QUANTITATIVE RESEARCH

Research can be qualitative or quantitative. Qualitative research is any kind of research whose data isn't in numerical form. This can include interviews, blog posts, Twitter posts, long-form log data, and long-form observations from ethnographers. Many people assume that survey research is qualitative because it doesn't come from computer systems, but that isn't necessarily true; it depends on the kinds of questions asked in the survey. Qualitative data is very descriptive and can allow for more insights and emergent behavior to be discovered by researchers, particularly in complex or new areas. However, it is often more difficult and costly to analyze; efforts to analyze qualitative data using automated means often codify the data into a numerical format, making it quantitative.

Quantitative research is any kind of research with data that includes numbers. These can include system data (in numerical format) or stock data. System data is any data generated from our tools; one example is log data. It can also include survey data, if the survey asks questions that capture responses in numerical format—preferably on a scale. The research presented in this book is quantitative, because it was collected using a Likert-type survey instrument.

What Is a Likert-Type Scale?

A Likert-type scale records responses and assigns them a number value. For example, "Strongly disagree" would be given a value of 1, neutral a value of 4, and "Strongly agree" a value of 7. This provides a consistent approach to measurement across all research subjects, and provides a numerical base for researchers to use in their analysis.

TYPES OF ANALYSIS

Quantitative research allows us to do statistical data analysis. According to a framework presented by Dr. Jeffrey Leek at Johns Hopkins Bloomberg School of Public Health (Leek 2013), there are six types of data analysis (given below in the order of increasing complexity). This complexity is due to the knowledge required by the data scientist, the costs involved in the analysis, and the time required to perform the analysis. These levels of analysis are:

1. Descriptive
2. Exploratory
3. Inferential predictive
4. Predictive
5. Causal
6. Mechanistic

The analyses presented in this book fall into the first three categories of Dr. Leek's framework. We also describe an additional type of analysis, classification, which doesn't fit cleanly into the above framework.

DESCRIPTIVE ANALYSIS

Descriptive analysis is used in census reports. The data is summarized and reported—that is, described. This type of analysis takes the least amount of effort, and is often done as the first step of data analysis to help the research team understand their dataset (and, by extension, their sample and possibly population of users). In some cases, a report will stop at descriptive analysis, as in the case of population census reports.

What Is a Population and Sample, and Why Are They Important?

When talking about statistics and data analysis, the terms "population" and "sample" have special meanings. The *population* is the entire group of something you are interested in researching; this might be all of the people undergoing technology transformations, everyone who is a Site Reliability

Engineer at an organization, or even every line in a log file during a certain time period. A *sample* is a portion of that population that is carefully defined and selected. The sample is the dataset on which researchers perform their analyses. Sampling is used when the entire population is too big or not easily accessible for research. Careful and appropriate sampling methods are important to make sure the conclusions drawn from analyzing the sample are true for the population.

The most common example of descriptive analysis is the government census where population statistics are summarized and reported. Other examples include most vendor and analyst reports that collect data and report summary and aggregate statistics about the state of tool usage in an industry or the level of education and certification among technology professionals. The percentage of firms that have started their Agile or DevOps journeys as reported by Forrester (Klavens et al. 2017), the IDC report on average downtime cost (Elliot 2014), and the O'Reilly Data Science Salary Survey (King and Magoulas 2016) belong in this category.

These reports are very useful as a gauge of the current state of the industry, where reference groups (such as populations or industries) currently are, where they once were, and where the trends are pointing. However, descriptive findings are only as good as the underlying research design and data collection methods. Any reports that aim to represent the underlying population must be sure to sample that population carefully and discuss any limitations. A discussion of these considerations is beyond the scope of this book.

An example of descriptive analysis found in this book is the demographic information about our survey participants and the organizations they work in—what countries they come from, how large their organizations are, the industry vertical they work in, their job titles, and their gender (see Chapter 10).

EXPLORATORY ANALYSIS

Exploratory analysis is the next level of statistical analysis. This is a broad categorization that looks for relationships among the data and may include visualizations to identify patterns in the data. Outliers may also be detected in this step, though the researchers have to be careful to make sure that outliers are, in fact, outliers, and not legitimate members of the group.

Exploratory analyses are a fun and exciting part of the research process. For those who are divergent thinkers, this is often the stage where new ideas, new hypotheses, and new research projects are generated and proposed. Here, we discover how the variables in our data are related and we look for possible new connections and relationships. However, this should not be the end for a team that wants to make statements about prediction or causation.

Many people have heard the phrase "correlation doesn't imply causation," but what does that mean? The analyses done in the exploratory stage include correlation but not causation. Correlation looks at how closely two variables move together—or don't—but it doesn't tell us if one variable's movement predicts or causes the movement in another variable. Correlation analysis only tells us if two variables move in tandem or in opposition; it doesn't tell us why or what is causing it. Two variables moving together can always be due to a third variable or, sometimes, just chance.

A fantastic and fun set of examples that highlight high correlations due to chance can be found at the website Spurious Correlations.[1] The author Tyler Vigen has calculated examples of highly correlated variables that common sense tells us are not predictive and certainly not causal. For example, he shows (Figure 12.1) that the per capita cheese consumption is highly correlated with the number of people who died by becoming tangled in their bedsheets (with a correlation of 94.71% or $r = 0.9471$; see footnote 2 on correlations in this chapter). Surely cheese consumption doesn't cause strangulation by bedsheets. (And if it does—what kind of cheese?) It would be just as difficult to imagine strangulation by bedsheets causing cheese consumption—unless that is the food of choice at funerals and wakes around the country. (And again: What kind of cheese? That is a morbid marketing opportunity.) And yet, when we go "fishing in the data," our minds fill in the story

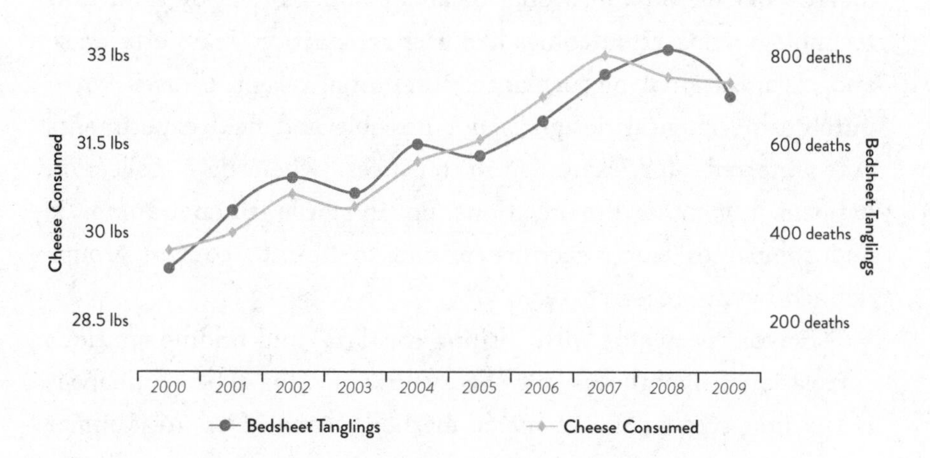

Figure 12.1: Spurious Correlation: Per Capita Cheese Consumption and Strangulation by Bedsheets

[1] http://www.tylervigen.com/spurious-correlations.

because our datasets are related and so often make sense. This is why it is so important to remember that correlation is only the exploratory stage: we can report correlations, and then we move on to more complex analyses.

There are several examples of correlations that are reported in our research and in this book, because we know the importance and value of understanding how things in our environment interrelate. In all cases, we reported Pearson correlations,[2] which is the correlation type most often used in business contexts today.

INFERENTIAL PREDICTIVE ANALYSIS

The third level of analysis, inferential, is one of the most common types conducted in business and technology research today. It is also called inferential predictive, and it helps us understand impacts of HR policies, organizational behavior and motivation, and how technology impacts outcomes like user satisfaction, team efficiency, and organizational performance. Inferential design is used when purely experimental design is not possible and field experiments are preferred—for example, in business, when data collection happens in complex organizations, not in sterile lab environments, and companies won't sacrifice profits to fit into control groups defined by the research team.

To avoid problems with "fishing for data" and finding spurious correlations, hypotheses are theory driven. This type of analysis is the first step in the scientific method. Many of us are familiar

---

[2] Pearson correlations measure the strength of a linear relationship between two variables, called Pearson's r. It is often referred to as just correlation and takes a value between -1 and 1. If two variables have a perfect linear correlation, that is they move together exactly, $r = 1$. If they move in exactly opposite directions, $r = -1$. If they are not correlated at all, $r = 0$.

with the scientific method: state a hypothesis and then test it. In this level of analysis, the hypothesis must be based on a well-developed and well-supported theory.

Whenever we talk about *impacting* or *driving* results in this book, our research design utilized this third type of analysis. While some suggest that using a theory-based design opens us up to confirmation bias, this is how science is done. Well, wait—almost. Science isn't done by simply confirming what the research team is looking for. Science *is* done by stating hypotheses, designing research to test those hypotheses, collecting data, and then testing the stated hypotheses. The more evidence we find to support a hypothesis, the more confidence we have for it. This process also helps to avoid the dangers that come from fishing for data—finding the spurious correlations that might randomly exist but have no real reason or explanation beyond chance.

Examples of hypotheses tested with inferential analysis in our project include continuous delivery and architecture practices driving software delivery performance, software delivery positively affecting organizational performance, and organizational culture having a positive impact on both software delivery and organizational performance. In these cases, the statistical methods used were either multiple linear regression or partial least squares regression. These methods are described in more detail in Appendix C.

PREDICTIVE, CAUSAL, AND MECHANISTIC ANALYSIS

The final levels of analysis were not included in our research, because we did not have the data necessary for this kind of work. We will briefly summarize them here for the sake of completeness and to appease your curiosity.

- Predictive analysis is used to predict, or forecast, future events based on previous events. Common examples include cost or utilities predictions in business. Prediction is very hard, particularly as you try to look farther away into the future. This analysis generally requires historical data.
- Causal analysis is considered the gold standard, but is more difficult than predictive analysis and is the most difficult analysis to conduct for most business and technology situations. This type of analysis generally requires randomized studies. A common type of casual analysis done in business is A/B testing in prototyping or websites, when randomized data can be collected and analyzed.
- Mechanistic analysis requires the most effort of all methods and is rarely seen in business. In this analysis, practitioners calculate the exact changes to make to variables to cause *exact* behaviors that will be observed under certain conditions. This is seen most often in the physical sciences or in engineering, and is not suitable for complex systems.

CLASSIFICATION ANALYSIS

Another type of analysis is classification, or clustering, analysis. Depending on the context, research design, and the analysis methods used, classification may be considered an exploratory, predictive, or even causal analysis. We use classification in this book when we talk about our high-, medium-, and low-performance software delivery teams. This may be familiar to you in other contexts when you hear about customer profiles or market basket analysis. At a high level, the process works like this: classification variables are entered into the clustering algorithm and significant groups are identified.

In our research, we applied this statistical method using the tempo and stability variables to help us understand and identify if there were differences in how teams were developing and delivering software, and what those differences looked like. Here is what we did: we put our four technology performance variables—deployment frequency, lead time for changes, mean time to repair, and change fail rate—into the clustering algorithm, and looked to see what groups emerged. We see distinct, statistically significant differences, where high performers do significantly better on all four measures, low performers perform significantly worse on all four measures, and medium performers are significantly better than low performers but significantly worse than high performers. For more detail, see Chapter 2.

What Is Clustering?

For those armchair (or professional) statisticians who are interested, we used hierarchical clustering. We chose this over k-means clustering for a few reasons. First, we didn't have any theoretical or other ideas about how many groups to expect prior to the analysis. Second, hierarchical clustering allowed us to investigate parent-child relationships in the emerging clusters, giving us greater interpretability. Finally, we didn't have a huge dataset, so computational power and speed wasn't a concern.

THE RESEARCH IN THIS BOOK

The research presented in this book covers a four-year time period, and was conducted by the authors. Because it is primary research, it is uniquely suited to address the research questions we had in mind—specifically, what capabilities drive software delivery performance and organizational performance? This project was based on quantitative survey data, allowing us to do statistical analyses to test our hypotheses and uncover insights into the factors that drive software delivery performance.

In the next chapters, we discuss the steps we took to ensure the data we collected from our surveys was good and reliable. Then, we look into why surveys may be a preferred source of data for measurement—both in a research project like ours and in your own systems.

CHAPTER 13

INTRODUCTION TO PSYCHOMETRICS

The two most common questions we get about our research are why we use surveys in our research (a question we will address in detail in the next chapter) and if we are sure we can trust data collected with surveys (as opposed to data that is system-generated). This is often fueled by doubts about the quality of our underlying data—and therefore, the trustworthiness of our results.

Skepticism about good data is valid, so let's start here: How much can you trust data that comes from a survey? Much of this concern comes from the types of surveys that many of us are exposed to: push polls (also known as propaganda surveys), quick surveys, and surveys written by those without proper research training.

Push polls are those with a clear and obvious agenda—their questions are difficult to answer honestly unless you already agree with the "researcher's" point of view. Examples are often seen in politics. For example, President Trump released his Mainstream Media Accountability Survey in February 2017, and the public quickly reacted with concern. Just a few highlights from the survey underscore concerns with the questions and their ability to gather data in a clear, unbiased way:

1. "Do you believe that the mainstream media has reported unfairly on our movement?" This was the first question in the survey and is subtle, but it sets the tone for the rest of the survey. By using the term "our movement," it invites the survey respondent into an *us vs. them* stance. "Mainstream media" is also a negatively charged term in this political cycle.
2. "Were you aware that a poll was released revealing that a majority of Americans actually supported President Trump's temporary restriction executive order?" This question is a clear example of push polling, where the question tries to give the survey respondent information rather than ask for their opinion or their perceptions about what is happening. The question also uses a psychological tactic, suggesting that "a majority of Americans" support the temporary restraining order, appealing to the reader's desire to belong to the group.
3. "Do you agree with President Trump's media strategy to cut through the media's noise and deliver our message straight to the people?" This question includes strong, polarizing language, characterizing all media as "noise"—a negative connotation in this political climate.

We can see in this example why people could be so skeptical of surveys. If this is your only exposure to them, of course they can't be trusted! No data from any of these questions can reliably tell what a person's perceptions or opinions are.

Even without an obvious example like push polling, bad surveys are found all over. Most often, they are the result of well-intentioned but untrained survey writers, hoping to gain some insight into their customers' or employees' opinions. Common weaknesses are:

- **Leading questions.** Survey questions should let the respondent answer without biasing them in a direction. For example, "How would you describe Napoleon's height?" is better than "Was Napoleon short?"
- **Loaded questions.** Questions should not force respondents into an answer that isn't true for them. For example, "Where did you take your certification exam?" doesn't allow for the possibility that they didn't take a certification exam.
- **Multiple questions in one.** Questions should only ask one thing. For example, "Are you notified of failures by your customers and the NOC?" doesn't tell you which part of the question your respondent was answering for. Customers? the NOC? Both? Or if no, neither?
- **Unclear language.** Survey questions should use language that your respondents are familiar with, and should clarify and provide examples when necessary.

A potential weakness of many survey questions used in business is that only a single question is used to collect data. Sometimes called "quick surveys," they are used quite often in marketing and business research. These can be useful if they are based on well-written and carefully understood questions. However, it is important that only narrow conclusions are drawn from these types of surveys. An example of a good quick survey is the Net Promoter Score (NPS). It has been carefully developed and studied, is well-understood, and its use and applicability are well-documented. Although better statistical measures of user and employee satisfaction exist, for example ones that use more questions (e.g., East et al. 2008), a single measure is often easier to get from your audience. Additionally, a benefit of NPS is that it has become an industry standard and is therefore easy to compare across teams and companies.

TRUSTING DATA WITH LATENT CONSTRUCTS

With all of these things to watch out for, how can we trust the data reported in survey measures? How can we be sure that someone lying on their survey won't skew the results? Our research uses latent constructs and statistical analyses to report good data—or at least provide a reasonable assurance that data is telling us what we think it's telling us.

A latent construct is a way of measuring something that can't be measured directly. We can ask for the temperature of a room or the response time of a website—these things we can measure directly.

A good example of something that can't be measured directly is organizational culture. We can't take a team's or an organization's organizational culture "temperature"—we need to measure culture by measuring its component parts (called manifest variables), and we measure these component parts through survey questions. That is, when you describe organizational culture of a team to someone, you probably include a handful of characteristics. Those characteristics are the component parts of organizational culture. We would measure each (as manifest variables), and together they would represent a team's organizational culture (the latent construct). And using survey questions to capture this data is appropriate, since culture is the lived experiences of those working on a team.

When working with latent constructs—or anything we want to measure in research—it is important to start with a clear definition and understanding of what it is we want to measure. In this case, we need to decide what we mean by "organizational culture." As we discuss in Chapter 3, the organizational culture that interested us was one that optimized trust and information flow. We referenced the typology proposed by Dr. Ron Westrum (2004), shown in Table 13.1.

Table 13.1 Westrum's Typology of Organizational Culture

Pathological (Power-Oriented)	Bureaucratic (Rule-Oriented)	Generative (Performance-Oriented)
Low cooperation	Modest cooperation	High cooperation
Messengers "shot"	Messengers neglected	Messengers trained
Responsibilities shirked	Narrow responsibilities	Risks are shared
Bridging discouraged	Bridging tolerated	Bridging encouraged
Failure leads to scapegoating	Failure leads to justice	Failure leads to enquiry
Novelty crushed	Novelty leads to problems	Novelty implemented

Once we have the construct identified, we write the survey questions. Clearly, the concept of organizational culture proposed by Dr. Westrum can't be captured in just a single question; organizational culture is a multifaceted idea. Asking someone "How is your organizational culture?" runs the risk of the question being understood differently by different people. By using latent constructs, we can ask one question for each aspect of the underlying idea. If we define the construct and write the items well, it works, conceptually, like a Venn diagram, with each survey question capturing a related aspect of the underlying concept.

After collecting the data, we can use statistical methods to verify that the measures do, in fact, reflect the core underlying concept. Once this is done, we can combine these measures to come up with a single number. In this example, the combination of the survey questions for each aspect of organizational culture becomes our measure for the concept. By averaging our scores on each item, we get an "organizational culture temperature" of sorts.

The benefit of latent constructs is that by using several measures (called manifest variables—the pieces of the latent variable that can be measured) to capture the underlying concept, you help shield yourself against bad measures and bad actors. How? This works in several ways, which are applicable to using system data to measure your system performance as well:

1. Latent constructs help us think carefully about what we want to measure and how we define our constructs.
2. They give us several views into the behavior and performance of the system we are observing, helping us eliminate rogue data.
3. They make it more difficult for a single bad data source (whether through misunderstanding or a bad actor) to skew our results.

LATENT CONSTRUCTS HELP US THINK CAREFULLY ABOUT WHAT WE'RE MEASURING

The first way that latent constructs help us avoid bad data is by helping us think carefully about what we want to measure and how we are defining our constructs. Taking time to think through this process can help us avoid bad measurements. Take a step back and think about *what* it is you are trying to measure and how you will measure, or proxy, it. Let's revisit our example of measuring culture.

We often hear that culture is important in technology transformations, so we want to measure it. Should we simply ask our employees and peers, "Is your culture good?" or "Do you like your team's culture?" And if they answered yes (or no), what would that even mean? What, exactly, would that tell us?

In the first question, what do we mean by culture, and how did the respondent interpret it? Which culture are we talking about: Your team's culture or your organization's culture? If we really are talking about a workplace culture, what aspects of this work culture are we referring to? Or are we really more interested in your national identity and culture? Assuming everyone understood the *culture* half of the question, what is *good*? Does good mean trusting? Fun? Or something else entirely? Is it even possible for a culture to be entirely good or entirely bad?

The second question is a bit better because we do specify that we're asking about culture at the team level. However, we still don't give the reader any idea of what we mean by "culture," so we can get data reflecting very different ideas of what *team culture* is. Another concern here is that we ask if the person *likes* their team culture. What does it mean to *like* a culture?

This may seem like an extreme example, but we see people make such mistakes all the time (although not you, dear reader). By taking a step back to think carefully about what you want to measure and by really defining what we mean by *culture*, we can get better data. When we hear that culture is important in technology transformations, we refer to a culture that has high trust, fosters information flow, builds bridges across teams, encourages novelty, and shares risks. With this definition of team and organizational culture in mind, we can see why the typology presented by Dr. Westrum was such a good fit for our research.

LATENT CONSTRUCTS GIVE US SEVERAL VIEWS INTO OUR DATA

The second way latent constructs help us avoid bad data is by giving us several views into the behavior and performance of the system we are observing. This lets us identify any rogue measures that would otherwise go undetected if they were the only measure we had to capture the behavior of the system.

Let's revisit the case of measuring organizational culture. To begin measuring this construct, we first proposed several aspects of organizational culture based on Dr. Westrum's definition. From these aspects, we wrote several items.[1] We will talk about writing good survey items and checking them for quality in more detail later in the chapter.

Once we collect the data, we can run several statistical tests to make sure that those items do, in fact, all measure the same underlying concept—the latent construct. These tests check for:

- **Discriminant validity:** tests to make sure that items that are not supposed to be related are actually unrelated (e.g., make sure that items that we believe are not capturing organizational culture are not, in fact, related to organizational culture).
- **Convergent validity:** tests to make sure that items that are supposed to be related are actually related (e.g., if items are supposed to measure organizational culture, then they do measure organizational culture).

[1] These are commonly referred to as survey questions. However, they aren't actually questions; instead, they are statements. We will refer to them as survey items in this book.

In addition to validity tests, reliability tests are conducted for our measures. This provides assurance that the items are read and interpreted similarly by those who take the survey. This is also referred to as internal consistency.

Taken together, validity and reliability statistical tests confirm our measures. They come before any analysis.

In the case of Westrum organizational culture, we have seven items that capture a team's organizational culture:

On my team . . .

- Information is actively sought.
- Messengers are not punished when they deliver news of failures or other bad news.
- Responsibilities are shared.
- Cross-functional collaboration is encouraged and rewarded.
- Failure causes inquiry.
- New ideas are welcomed.
- Failures are treated primarily as opportunities to improve the system.

Using a scale from "1 = Strongly disagree" to "7 = Strongly agree," teams can quickly and easily measure their organizational culture.

These items have been tested and found to be statistically valid and reliable. That is, they measure the things they are intended to measure, and people generally read and interpret them consistently. You'll also notice that we asked these items for a *team* and not for an organization. We made this decision when creating the survey items—as a departure from Westrum's original framework—because organizations can be very large and can have pockets of different organizational cultures. In addition, people can answer more accurately for their team than for their organization. This helps us collect better measures.

LATENT CONSTRUCTS HELP SAFEGUARD AGAINST ROGUE DATA

This deserves a slight clarification. Latent constructs *that are periodically retested with statistics and exhibit good psychometric properties* help us safeguard against rogue data.

What? Let us explain.

In the previous section, we talked about validity and reliability—statistical tests we can do to make sure the survey items that measure a latent construct belong together. When our constructs pass all of these statistical tests, we say they "exhibit good psychometric properties." It's a good idea to reassess these periodically to make sure nothing has changed, especially if you suspect a change in the system or environment.

In the organizational culture example, all of the items are good measures of the construct. Here is another example of a construct where tests highlighted opportunities to improve our measure. In this case, we were interested in examining failure notification. The items were:

- We are primarily notified of failures by reports from customers.
- We are primarily notified of failures by the NOC.
- We get failure alerts from logging and monitoring systems.
- We monitor system health based on threshold warnings (ex. CPU exceeds 90%).

- We monitor system health based on rate-of-change warnings (ex. CPU usage has increased by 25% over the last 10 minutes).

In preliminary survey design, we pilot-tested the construct with about 20 technical professionals and the items loaded together (that is, they measured the same underlying construct). However, when we completed our final, larger data collection, we did tests to confirm the construct. In these final tests, we found that these items actually measured two different things. That is, when we ran our statistical tests, they did not confirm a single construct, but instead revealed two constructs. The first two items measure one construct, which appears to capture "notifications that come from outside of automated processes":

- We are primarily notified of failures by reports from customers.
- We are primarily notified of failures by the NOC.

The second set of items capture another construct—"notifications that come from systems" or "proactive failure notification":

- We get failure alerts from logging and monitoring systems.
- We monitor system health based on threshold warnings (ex. CPU exceeds 90%).
- We monitor system health based on rate-of-change warnings (ex. CPU usage has increased by 25% over the last 10 minutes).

If we had only asked our survey respondents if they monitor for failures with a single survey question, we would not be aware of the importance of capturing *where* these notifications come from. Furthermore, if one of these notification sources alters its behavior, our statistical tests will catch it and alert us. The same concept can apply to system data. We can use multiple measures from our systems to capture system behavior, and these measures can pass our validity checks. However, we should continue to do periodic checks on these measures because they can change.

Our research found that this second construct, proactive failure notification, is a technical capability that is predictive of software delivery performance.

HOW LATENT CONSTRUCTS CAN BE USED FOR SYSTEM DATA

Some of these ideas about latent constructs extend to system data as well: They help us avoid bad data by using several measures to look for similar patterns of behavior, and they help us think through what it is we are really trying to proxy. For example, let's say we want to measure system performance. We can simply collect response time of some aspect of the system. To look for similar patterns in the data, we can collect several pieces of data from our system that can help us understand its response time. To think about what we are truly trying to measure—performance—we can consider various aspects of performance, and how else it might be reflected in system metrics. We might realize that we are interested in a conceptual measure of system performance which is difficult to measure directly and is better captured through several related measures.

There is one important note to make here: all measures are proxies. That is, they represent an idea to us, even if we don't acknowledge it consciously. This is just as true of system data as it is of survey data. For example, we may use response time as a proxy for performance of our system.

If only one of the data points is used as the barometer and that one data point is bad—or goes bad—we won't know it. For example, a change to source code that collects metrics can affect one measure; if only that single measure is collected, the likelihood of us catching the change is low. However, if we collect several metrics, this change in behavior has a better chance of being detected. Latent constructs give us one mechanism to protect ourselves against bad measures or bad agents. This is true in both surveys and system data.

CHAPTER 14

WHY USE A SURVEY

Now that we know our survey data can be trusted—that is, we have a reasonable assurance that data from our well-designed and well-tested psychometric survey constructs is telling us what we think it's telling us—why would we use a survey? And why should anyone else use a survey? Teams wanting to understand the performance of their software delivery process often begin by instrumenting their delivery process and toolchain to obtain data (we call data gathered in this way "system data" throughout this book). Indeed, several tools on the market now offer analysis on items such as lead time. Why would someone want to collect data from surveys and not just from your toolchain?

There are several reasons to use survey data. We'll briefly present some of these in this chapter.

1. Surveys allow you to collect and analyze data quickly.
2. Measuring the full stack with system data is difficult.
3. Measuring completely with system data is difficult.
4. You can trust survey data.
5. Some things can only be measured through surveys.

SURVEYS ALLOW YOU TO COLLECT AND ANALYZE DATA QUICKLY

Often, the strongest reason to use surveys is speed and ease of data collection. This is particularly true for new or one-time data collection efforts, or for data collection that spans or crosses organizational boundaries. The research that appears in this book was collected four different times.

Each time, we gathered data over a four- to six-week period, from around the world, and from thousands of survey respondents representing thousands of organizations. Imagine the difficulty (in reality, the impossibility) of getting system data from that many teams in that same time period. Just the legal clearances would be impossible, let alone the data specifications and transfer.

But let's assume we were able to collect system data from a few thousand respondents from around the world in a four-week window. The next step is data cleaning and analysis. Data analysis for the State of DevOps Reports is generally 3–4 weeks. Many of you have probably worked with system data; even more of you have probably had the distinct pleasure (more likely pain) of combining and collating Excel spreadsheets. Imagine getting rough system data (or maybe capital planning spreadsheets) from several thousand teams from around the world. Imagine the challenge to clean, organize, and then analyze this data, and be prepared to deliver results for reporting in three weeks.

In addition to the basic challenge of cleaning the data and running the analyses lies a significant challenge that can call into question all of your work, and is probably the biggest constraint: the data itself. More specifically, the underlying *meaning* of the data itself.

You've probably seen it in your own organizations: Different teams can refer to very different (or even slightly different) measures by the same name. Two examples are "lead time" (which we define as the time from code commit to code in a deployable state) and "cycle time" (which some define as the time from code starting to be worked on by development to code in a deployable state). However, these two terms are often used interchangeably and are quite often confused, though they measure different things.

So what happens if one team calls it cycle time and the other team calls it lead time—but they both measure the same thing? Or what if they both call it lead time but are measuring two different things? And then we have collected the data and are trying to run the analysis . . . but we do not know for certain which variables are which? This poses significant measurement and analysis problems.

Carefully worded and crafted surveys that have been vetted help solve this problem. All respondents are now working from the same items, the same words, and the same definitions. It doesn't matter what they call it at their organization—it matters what they have been asked in the survey. It *does* matter what they are asked, and so the quality and clarity of the survey items become that much more important. But once the work of survey writing is done, the work of cleaning and preparing the data for analysis is faster and more straightforward.

In rigorous research, additional analyses (e.g., common method variance checks) are run to ensure that the survey itself hasn't introduced bias into the results, and responses are checked for bias between early and late responders (see Appendix C).

MEASURING THE FULL STACK WITH SYSTEM DATA IS DIFFICULT

Even if your system is reporting out good and useful data (an assumption that we know from experience is quite often wrong and generally needs to be ascertained by trial and error), that data is rarely exhaustive. That is, can you really be sure it's measuring 100% of the system's behavior you're interested in?

Let's illustrate this with an example. One of the authors spent a portion of her career as a performance engineer at IBM, working on enterprise disk storage systems. Her team's role was to diagnose and optimize the performance of these machines, including disk read, write, cache, and RAID rebuild operations over various workload conditions. After working through several initiatives, "the box" was performing well, and the team had the metrics from all levels of the system to prove it. Occasionally, the team would still hear back from customers that the box was slow. The team always investigated—but the first report or two was dismissed by the team because they had confirmation that the performance of the box was good: all of the system logs showed it!

However, as the team started getting more reports of slow performance, more investigation was necessary. Sure, customers and the field could have incentive to lie, for example for discounts based on broken SLAs. But the customer and field reports had a pattern—they all showed similar slowness. While this data-from-people didn't have the same degree of precision as the system logs (e.g., the minute-level precision in the reported response times vs. the millisecond precision from log files), this gave the team enough data to know where to look. It suggested patterns and showed a signal to follow in their work.

So what was it? It turned out that the box itself was performing exceptionally well. The team *had* instrumented every level of the stack and were capturing everything there was to capture . . . *in the box*. What the team hadn't captured was the interface. The way that customers were interacting with the box was introducing significant performance degradations. The team quickly spun up a small group to address and manage this new area, and soon the full system was operating at peak performance.

Without asking *people* about the performance of the system, the team would not have understood what was going on. Taking time to do periodic assessments that include the perceptions of the technologists that make and deliver your technology can uncover key insights into the bottlenecks and constraints in your system. By surveying everyone on your team, you can help avoid problems associated with having a few overly positive or overly negative responses.[1]

MEASURING COMPLETELY WITH SYSTEM DATA IS DIFFICULT

A related reason for using surveys is the inability to capture everything that is happening through system data—because your systems only know about what is happening inside the system boundaries. Conversely, people can see everything happening in and around the system and report about it. Let's illustrate with an example.

---

[1] This, of course, assumes that you collect the data with an eye toward improvement—without telling everyone they must answer positively *or else*. That would be the equivalent of the joke: "Beatings will continue until morale improves." You would get the data you want—good responses—but it would be meaningless. One way to help encourage honest responses is to ensure anonymous data collection.

Our research has found that the use of version control is a key capability in software delivery performance. If we want to know the extent to which a team is using version control for all production artifacts, we can ask the team. They can tell us because they have the visibility to all of the work. However, if we want to measure this through the system, we have significant limitations. The system can only tell us what it sees—how many files or repositories are being checked in to version control. But this raw number isn't meaningful without context.

Ideally, we would like to know the percentage of files or repos that are in version control—but the system can't tell us that: it would require counting files checked in as well as files *not* checked in, and the system does not know how many files are not in version control. A system only has visibility to things in it—in this case, the use of version control systems is something that can't be accurately measured from log files and instrumentation.

People won't have perfect knowledge or visibility into systems either—but if you ignore the perceptions and experience of the professionals working on your systems entirely, you lose an important view into your systems.

YOU CAN TRUST SURVEY DATA

We are often asked how we can trust any data that comes from surveys—and, by extension, the findings that come from surveys. This may be illustrated by a thought exercise that we use sometimes when addressing groups of technologists and asking about their work. Ask yourself (or someone you know who works in software development and delivery) these questions:

1. **Do you trust survey data?** Without fail, this first question gets very little support; many in our audience sadly assume the worst in people and expect them to lie in surveys, or they expect survey writers and designers to try to "game" the questions to get the results they want—a topic we covered earlier.
2. **Do you trust your system or log data?** On this second question, there is often more support and nodding heads. We are comfortable with the data that comes from our systems because we feel confident that it hasn't been tampered with. So, we move on to our third question.
3. **Have you ever seen bad data come from your system?** In our experience, almost everyone has seen bad data in system files. While many assume the system data hasn't been tampered with, humans make systems (and therefore the data that comes from systems) and humans make mistakes. Or, if we do assume that bad actors can exist in our systems, it takes only one bad actor to introduce code that will make the system give us erroneous data.

Bad Actors and System Data

The cult classic *Office Space* is built around this premise: A bad actor introduces changes to financial software that deposits very small amounts of money (referred to as a "rounding error") to a personal account. This rounding error is then not reported on financial reports. This is an excellent example of bad system data.

If we are so familiar with bad data in our systems, why are we so trusting of that data and yet so skeptical of survey data? Perhaps it is because as engineers and technicians, we understand how our systems work. We believe we will be able to spot the errors in the data that come from these systems, and when we do, we will know how to fix it.

In contrast, working with survey data seems foreign, especially for those who have not been trained in survey writing and psychometric methods. But a review of the concepts presented in Part II of the book should demonstrate that there are steps that can be taken to make our survey data more reliable. These include the use of carefully identified measures, latent constructs, and statistical methods to confirm the validity and reliability of measures.

Compare our two cases: system data and survey data. In the case of system data, one or a few people can change the data reported in log files. This can be a highly motivated bad actor with root (or high system) access, or it can be a developer who made a mistake and whose error isn't caught by a review or test. Their impact on the data quality is significant, because you probably only have one or a few data points that the business pays attention to. In this case, your raw data is bad, and you might not catch it for months or years, if at all.

In the case of survey data, a few highly motivated bad actors can lie on survey questions, and their responses may skew the results of the overall group. Their impact on the data depends on the size of the group surveyed. In the research conducted for this book, we have over 23,000 respondents whose responses are pooled together. It would take several hundred people "lying" in a coordinated, organized way to make a noticeable difference—that is, they would need to lie about every item in the latent construct to the same degree in the same direction. In this case, the use of a survey actually protects us against bad actors. There are additional steps taken to ensure good data is collected; for example, all responses are anonymous, which helps people who take the survey feel safe to respond and share honest feedback.

This is why we can trust the data in our survey—or at least have a reasonable assurance that the data is telling us what we think it is telling us: we use latent constructs and write our survey measures carefully and thoughtfully, avoiding the use of any propaganda items; we perform several statistical tests to confirm that our measures meet psychometric standards for validity and reliability; and we have a large dataset that pulls respondents from around the world, which serves as a safeguard against errors or bad actors.

SOME THINGS CAN ONLY BE MEASURED THROUGH SURVEYS

There are some things that can only be measured using surveys. When we want to ask about perceptions, feelings, and opinions, using surveys is often the only way to do this. We will again point to our previous example of organizational culture.

Often, people will want to defer to objective data to proxy for something like organizational culture. Objective data is not influenced by feelings or emotions; in contrast, subjective data captures one's perceptions or feelings about a situation. In the case of organizational culture, teams often look to objective measures because they want a faster way to collect the data (for example, from HR systems), and there is still a worry about people lying about their feelings. The challenge with using variables that exist in HR systems to proxy for "culture" is that these variables are rarely a direct mapping. For example, a commonly used metric for a "good" organizational culture is retention—or in reverse, the metric for a "bad" organizational culture is turnover.

There are several problems with this proxy because there are many factors that influence whether or not someone stays with a team or an organization. For example:

- If an employee receives an offer from another firm for a significant pay increase and leaves, their turnover may have nothing to do with the culture.
- If an employee's spouse or partner receives a job offer that requires relocation and your employee decides to follow them, their turnover probably has nothing to do with culture.
- If an employee decides to pursue a different career or return to school, this may have nothing to do with the culture and more to do with their personal journey. In fact, one of the authors knows of a case where an employee worked at a very supportive, encouraging company and on a great team. It was that great team environment that encouraged him to follow his dreams and pursue a change in career so he could continue being challenged. In this case, the strong culture resulted in turnover, not the opposite.
- These measures can be gamed. If an employee's manager finds out they are actively looking for a job, the manager may lay the person off to make sure the employee is not counted in any turnover numbers. And in the reverse, if managers are rewarded for retaining team members, they may block transfers off of their teams, retaining people even when their team culture is bad.

Turnover can be a useful measure if we think carefully about what we're measuring.[2] But in the examples above, we see that employee turnover and retention don't tell us much about our team or organizational culture—or if they do, it's not what we may think. If we want to understand how people feel about taking risks, sharing information, and communicating across boundaries, we have to ask them. Yes, you can use other system proxies to see some of these things happening; for example, you can observe network traffic to see which team members communicate with each other more often, and you can observe trends over time to see if team members are communicating more or less often. You can even run semantic analysis to see if the words in their emails or chats are generally positive or negative. But if you want to know how they *feel* about the work environment and how supportive it is to their work and their goals—if you want to know *why* they're behaving in the way you observe—you have to ask them. And the best way to do that in a systematic, reliable way that can be compared over time is through surveys.

And it is worth asking. Research has shown that organizational culture is predictive of technology and organizational performance, is predictive of performance outcomes, and that team dynamics and psychological safety are the most important aspects in understanding team performance (Google 2015).

[2] For an interesting example of using retention as a way to determine the effectiveness of the interview process, see Kahneman 2011.

CHAPTER 15

THE DATA FOR THE PROJECT

This project started with a desire to understand how to make technology great and how technology makes organizations better. Specifically, we wanted to investigate the new ways, methods, and paradigms that organizations were using to develop and deliver software, with a focus on Agile and Lean processes that extended downstream from development and prioritized a culture of trust and information flow, with small cross-functional teams creating software. At the beginning of the project in 2014, this development and delivery methodology was widely known as "DevOps," and so this was the term we used.

Our research design—a cross-sectional data collection[1] for four years—recruited professionals and organizations familiar with the word DevOps (or at least willing to read an email or social media post with the word DevOps), which targeted our data collection accordingly. Any good research design defines a target population, and this was ours. We chose this strategy for two primary reasons:

---

[1] A cross-sectional design means the data was collected at a single point in time. However, it precluded us from longitudinal analysis because our responses are not linked year over year. By repeating the study over four years, we were able to observe patterns across the industry. While we would like to collect a longitudinal data set—that is, one where we sample the *same* individuals year over year—this could reduce response rates due to privacy concerns. (And what happens when those people change teams or jobs?) We are currently pursuing research in this area. Cross-sectional research design does have its benefits: data collection at a single point in time reduces variability in the research design.

1. **It allowed us to focus our data collection.** In this research, the users were those who were in the business of software development and delivery, whether their parent organization's industry was technology or was driven by technology, such as retail, banking, telecommunications, healthcare, or several other industries.
2. **It allowed us to focus on users who were relatively familiar with DevOps concepts.** Our research targeted users already familiar with terminology used by technology professionals who use more modern software development and delivery practices, whether or not they identified as DevOps practitioners. This was important, because time and space were limited, and too much time spent on background definitions and a long explanation of concepts, such as continuous integration and configuration management, could risk survey respondents opting out of the study. If a survey reader has to spend 15 minutes learning about a concept in order to answer questions about it, they will get frustrated and annoyed and won't complete the survey.

This targeted research design was a strength for our research. No research design is able to answer all questions, and all design decisions involve trade-offs. We did not collect data from professionals and organizations who were not familiar with things like configuration management, infrastructure-as-code, and continuous integration. By not collecting data on this group, we miss a cohort that are likely performing even worse than our low performers. This means our comparisons are limited and we don't discover the truly compelling and drastic transformations that are possible. However, we gain explanatory power by limiting the population to those that fall into a tighter group definition. That increase in explanatory power comes at the expense of capturing and analyzing the behaviors of those that do not use modern technology practices to make and maintain software.

This data selection and research design did require some caution. By only surveying those familiar with DevOps, we had to be careful in our wording. That is, some who responded to our survey might want to paint their team or organization in a favorable light, or they might have their own definition of key terms. For example, everyone knows (or claims to know) what continuous integration (CI) is, and many organizations claim CI as a core competency. Therefore, we never asked any respondents in our surveys if they practiced continuous integration. (At least, we didn't ask in any questions about CI that would be used for any prediction analysis.) Instead, we would ask about practices that are a core aspect of CI, e.g. if automated tests are kicked off when code is checked in. This helped us avoid bias that could creep in by targeting users that were familiar with DevOps.

However, based on prior research, our own experiences, and the experiences of those who have led technology transformations in large enterprises, we believe that many of our findings are broadly applicable to teams and organizations undergoing transformations. For example, the use of version control and automated testing is highly likely to yield positive results, whether a team is using DevOps practices, Agile methodologies, or hoping to improve their lockstep waterfall development methods. Similarly, having an organizational culture that values transparency, trust, and innovation is likely to have positive impacts in technology organizations regardless of software development paradigm—and in any industry vertical, since that framework is predictive of performance outcomes in different contexts, including healthcare and aviation.

Once we defined our target population, we decided on a sampling method: How would we invite people to take the survey? There are two broad categories of sampling methods: probability sampling and nonprobability sampling.[2] We were not able to use probability sampling methods because this would require that every member of the population is known and has an equal chance of participating in the study. This isn't possible because an exhaustive list of DevOps professionals in the world doesn't exist. We explain this in more detail below.

To collect the data for our research, we sent out emails and used social media. Emails were sent to our own mailing lists, which consisted of technologists and professionals who worked in DevOps (e.g., were in our database because they had participated in prior years' studies, were in Puppet's marketing databases because of their work with configuration management, were in Gene Kim's database because of their interest in his books and work in the industry, or were in Jez Humble's database because of their interest in his books and work in the industry). Emails were also sent to mailing lists for professional groups. Special care was also taken to send invitations to groups that included underrepresented groups and minorities in technology. In addition to direct invitations by email, we leveraged social media, with authors and survey sponsors tweeting links to the survey and posting links to take the survey on LinkedIn. By inviting survey participation from several sources, we increased our chances of exposure to more DevOps professionals while addressing limitations of snowball sampling, discussed below.

[2] Probability sampling is any method of statistical sampling that uses random selection; by extension, nonprobability sampling is any method that does not use random selection. Random selection ensures that all individuals in a population have an equal chance of being selected in the sample. Therefore, probability sampling is generally preferred. However, probability sampling methods are not always possible because of environmental or contextual factors.

To expand our reach into the technologists and organizations developing and delivering software, we also invited referrals. This aspect of growing our initial sample is called referral sampling or snowball sampling because the sample grows by picking up additional respondents as it spreads, just like a snowball grows as you roll it through the snow. Snowball sampling was an appropriate data collection method for this study for several reasons:

- **Identifying the population of those who make software using DevOps methodologies is difficult or impossible.** Unlike professional organizations like accounting or civil engineering, which in the US have national certifications such as CPA (Certified Public Accountants) or PE (Practice of Engineering), there is no central accrediting board that could give us a list of professionals to reference. Beyond this, we could not scour organization charts (even if they were publicly available) for job titles as not everyone has "DevOps" or other important keywords in their job title. In addition, many technologists, especially at the beginning of the research project, had nontraditional job titles. Even if organization charts were public, many job titles are too generic to be useful for recruitment in the study (such as "software engineer," which can include developers working in teams using waterfall or DevOps methods). Snowball sampling is a method well suited for studying specific groups whose populations cannot be easily identified.
- **The population is typically and traditionally averse to being studied.** There is a strong (and unfortunate) history of organizational studies of technical workers leading to "Lean transformations" which really just mean a significant workforce reduction. Snowball sampling is a method that is

ideal for populations that are often averse to being studied; by referring others to the study, they can vouch for the questions (reassuring the new participant that the questions are not propaganda) or even for the reputation of the researchers.

There are some limitations inherent in snowball sampling. The first limitation is the potential that the initial users sampled (in our case, emailed) are not representative of the communities they belong to. We compensated for this by having an initial set of invitations (or informants) that was as large and as diverse as possible. We did this by combining several mailing lists, including our own survey mailing list, which had a diverse set of respondents covering a large variation from company size and countries. We also reached out to underrepresented groups and minorities in technology through their own mailing lists and organizations.

Another limitation of snowball sampling is that the data collected is strongly influenced by the initial invitations. This is a concern if only a small group of people are targeted and then asked for referrals, and the sample grows from there. We addressed this limitation by inviting a very large and diverse group of people to participate in the study, as described above.

Finally, there may be a concern that findings will not be representative of what is actually happening in the industry, that we may have blind spots that we do not see in our data. We address this in a few ways. First, we do not simply rely on the research results each year to inform our conclusions; we actively engage with the industry and the community to make sure we know what is happening, and triangulate our results with emerging trends. That means we actively seek feedback on our survey, through the community at conferences, and through colleagues and the industry; we then compare notes to see what trends are emerging, never relying on only one data source. If any discrepancies or mismatches occur, we revisit our hypotheses and iterate. Second, we have external subject matter experts in the industry review our hypotheses each year to ensure we are current. Third, we explore the existing literature to look for patterns in other fields that may provide insights into our study. Finally, we ask for input and research ideas from the community each year and use these ideas when we design the research.

PART THREE
TRANSFORMATION

We've presented our findings on which capabilities are important in producing better software delivery and organizational outcomes. However, taking this information and applying it to change your organization is a complex and daunting task. That's why we're delighted that Steve Bell and Karen Whitley Bell agreed to write a chapter on leadership and organizational transformation, sharing their experience and insights to guide readers in their own journey.

Steve and Karen are pioneers of Lean IT, applying principles and practices through a method-agnostic approach, drawing on a variety of practices—DevOps, Agile, Scrum, kanban, Lean startup, Kata, Obeya, strategy deployment, and others—as appropriate to the culture and situation, to coach and support leaders to develop high-performance practices and organizational learning capabilities.

In Part III, they draw on their experiences at ING Netherlands, a global bank with over 34.4 million customers worldwide and with 52,000 employees, including more than

9,000 engineers, to show the why and how of leadership, management, and team practices that enable culture change. This, in turn, enables sustainable high performance in a complex and dynamic environment.

Steve and Karen extend our view beyond the interrelationships of team, management, and leadership practices, beyond the skillful adoption of DevOps, and beyond the breaking down of silos—all necessary, but not sufficient. Here we see the evolution of holistic, end-to-end organizational transformation, fully engaged and fully aligned to enterprise purpose.

CHAPTER 16

HIGH-PERFORMANCE LEADERSHIP AND MANAGEMENT

By Steve Bell and Karen Whitley Bell

"Leadership really does have a powerful impact on results. . . . A good leader affects a team's ability to deliver code, architect good systems, and apply Lean principles to how the team manages its work and develops products. All of these," the research shows, "have a measurable impact on an organization's profitability, productivity, and market share. These also have an impact on customer satisfaction, efficiency, and the ability to achieve organizational goals."[1] Yet, Nicole, Jez, and Gene also observe that "the role of leadership on technology transformation has been one of the more overlooked topics in DevOps."

Why is that? Why have technology practitioners continuously sought to improve the approach to software development and deployment as well as the stability and security of infrastructure and platforms, yet, in large part, have overlooked (or are unclear about) the way to lead, manage, and sustain these endeavors? This holds

[1] See Chapter 11, pp. 115–116.

for large legacy enterprises as well as digital natives. Let's consider this question not in the context of the past—why we haven't—but instead for the present and future: why we must improve the way we lead and manage IT[2] and, indeed, reimagine the way everyone across the enterprise views and engages with technology.

We are in the midst of a complete transformation in the way value is created, delivered, and consumed. Our ability to rapidly and effectively envision, develop, and deliver technology-related value to enhance the customer experience is becoming a key competitive differentiator. But peak technical performance is only one part of competitive advantage—necessary but not sufficient. We may become great at rapidly developing and delivering reliable, secure, technology-enabled experiences, but how do we know which experiences our customers value? How do we prioritize what we create so that each team's efforts advance the larger enterprise strategy? How do we learn from our customers, from our actions, and from each other? And as we learn, how do we share that learning across the enterprise and leverage that learning to continuously adapt and innovate?

The other necessary component to sustaining competitive advantage is a lightweight, high-performance management framework that connects enterprise strategy with action, streamlines the flow of ideas to value, facilitates rapid feedback and learning, and capitalizes on and connects the creative capabilities of every individual throughout the enterprise to create optimal customer experiences. What does such a framework look like—not in theory but in practice? And how do we go about improving and transforming our own leadership, management, and team practices and behaviors to become the enterprise we aspire to be?

---

[2] Note from Nicole, Jez, and Gene. The term "IT" is used throughout this chapter to refer to the software and technology process—much more than just a single function within the technology group at a company, like IT support or the helpdesk.

A HIGH-PERFORMING MANAGEMENT FRAMEWORK IN PRACTICE

Throughout this book, Nicole, Jez, and Gene discuss several Lean management practices that have been found to correlate with high organizational performance—specifically, "profitability, market share, and productivity . . . [in addition to measures that capture] broader organizational goals—that is, goals that go beyond simple profit and revenue measures."[3] Each of these practices is, in some way, synergistic and interdependent with the others. To illustrate how these leadership, management, and team practices work together, and to show the foundational thinking that enables them, we share the experiences of ING Netherlands, a global financial institution that pioneered digital banking and is recognized for its customer-centric technology leadership. Today, IT is leading ING's digital transformation effort.

"You have to understand why, not just copy the behaviors,"[4] says Jannes Smit, IT Manager of Internet Banking and Omnichannel at ING Netherlands, who, seven years ago, decided to experiment with ways to develop organizational learning among his teams. There are many ways we could describe this management practice in action. Perhaps the best way is to take you on a virtual visit—albeit from the pages of a book. (ING is happy to share the story of their learning, but they're not willing to show you what's on the walls!) We'll share with you the sights and sounds and experiences of a day at ING, showing you how practices, rhythms, and routines connect to create a learning organization and deliver high performance and value.

---

[3] See Chapter 2, p. 24.

[4] This and all other direct quotes from ING staff are personal communications with the authors of this chapter.

What you see today bears little resemblance to what we first observed as we periodically visited to facilitate what they called "boot camps" to rethink how Jannes and his managers led and managed teams. Like many enterprise IT organizations, they were located offsite from the main campus and were viewed by many as a function rather than as a vital contributor in realizing enterprise strategy. Today, we enter at the main corporate headquarters, where Jannes' teams are now located one floor below the C-suite. The space is open and light. After security, we pass through a large, open social area—coffee bars and snack kiosks overlooking gardens—designed to create intimate spaces to gather, visit, and share ideas. We then enter the Tribe's suite. Immediately to our left is a large room with glass walls, creating visibility to the space within. This is the Obeya room where the Tribe lead's work, priorities, and action items are visualized for the teams and anyone else who may schedule a meeting in this space or visit between meetings to update or review status. Here Jannes meets on a regular cadence with his direct reports, where they can quickly see and understand the status of each of his strategic objectives. Four distinct zones are visualized: strategic improvement, performance monitoring, portfolio roadmap, and leadership actions, each with current information about targets, gaps, progress, and problems. Color coding is used—red and green—to make problems immediately visible. Each IT objective ties directly, in measurable ways, to enterprise strategy (see Figure 16.1).

Figure 16.1: Leadership Obeya (360-Degree Panorama)

Two years ago, ING underwent a significant shift to a multi-dimensional, matrixed structure organized along lines of business, enabling the continuous flow of customer value (what Lean practitioners call value streams). Each line of business is organized as a tribe delivering a portfolio of related products and services (for example, the Mortgage Services Tribe). Each tribe is comprised of multiple self-steering teams, called squads, each responsible for a distinct customer mission (for example, the Mortgage Application Squad). Each squad is guided by a product owner, led (in case of IT) by an IT-area lead, and sized according to Bezos' Two Pizza Rule—no team can be so large that it would require more than two pizzas to feed them. Most squads are cross-functional, consisting of engineers and marketers, collaborating as a single team with a shared understanding of customer value. At ING, this team composition is referred to as BizDevOps. Recently, they identified a need for a new bridging structure which they plan to call a product area lead, to align multiple, closely related squads. This new role wasn't planned—it emerged through experience and learning. There are also chapters, comprised of members of the same discipline (for example, the Data Analytics Chapter), who are matrixed across squads and bring specialized knowledge to promote learning and advancement among squad members. And finally, there are centers of expertise, bringing together individuals with particular capabilities (for example, communications or enterprise architects—see Figure 16.2).

We move on from Jannes' Obeya, accompanied by Jannes' internal continuous improvement coaches: David Bogaerts, Jael Schuyer, Paul Wolhoff, Liedewij van der Scheer, and Ingeborg Ten Berge. Together, they form a small but effective Lean Leadership Expertise Squad and coach the leaders, chapter leads, product

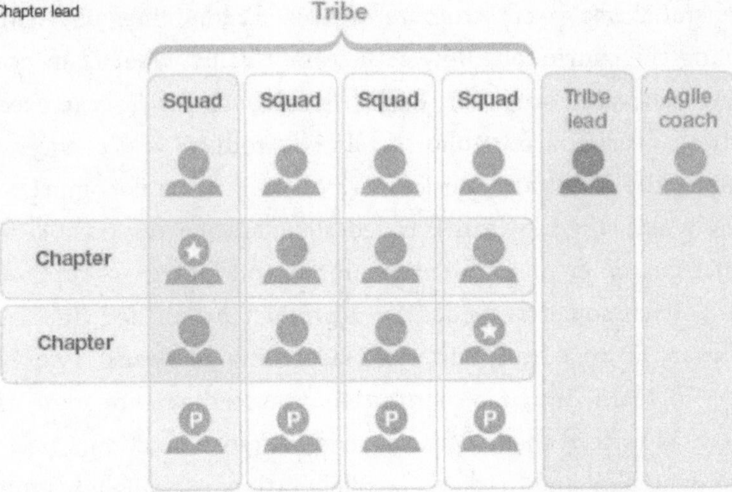

Tribe

(collection of squads with interconnected missions)

- includes on average 150 people
- empowers tribe lead to establish priorities, allocate budgets, and form interface with other tribes to ensure knowledge/insights are shared

Agile coach

- coaches individuals and squads to create high-performing teams

Squad

(basis of new agile organization)

- includes no more than 9 people; is self-steering and autonomous
- comprises representatives of different functions working in single location
- has end-to-end responsibility for achieving client-related objective
- can change functional composition as mission evolves
- is dismantled as soon as mission is executed

Product owner

(squad member, not its leader)

- is responsible for coordinating squad activities
- manages backlog, to-do lists, and priority setting

Chapter

(develops expertise and knowledge across squads)

Chapter lead

- is responsible for one chapter
- represents hierarchy for squad members (re: personal development, coaching, staffing, and performance management)

Figure 16.2: ING's New Agile Organizational Model Has No Fixed Structure—It Constantly Evolves. (Source ING)

owners, and IT-area leads who, in turn, coach their chapter or squad members, creating a leveraged effect to change behavior and culture at scale.

Just ahead is a squad workspace—an open area with windows and walls that are covered in visuals (their own Obeya) that enable the squad to monitor performance in real time, and see obstacles, status of improvements, and other information of value to the squad. Across the middle of the space flows a row of adjustable-height tables, with adjustable-height chairs, enabling squad members to sit or stand, facing each other across their screens. The chairs are of different shapes and colors, making the space visually interesting and ergonomically sound. Squad visuals share some characteristics; the similarities in Obeya design enable colleagues outside the squad to immediately understand, at a glance, certain aspects of the work, promoting shared learning. Standard guidelines include visualizing goals, present performance and gaps, new and escalated problems, demand, WIP, and done work. Visualizing demand helps prioritize and keep the WIP load small. The visuals also have some differences, recognizing that the work of each squad is somewhat unique and each squad is the best judge of what information—and what visualization of that information—best serves them to excel at their work.

As we pass through, the squad is conducting its daily stand-up, where rapid learning and feedback takes place. Standing in front of a visual board displaying demand and WIP, each member briefly reports what she/he is working on (WIP), any obstacles, and what has been completed. As they speak, the visual is updated. These stand-ups usually last around 15 minutes; they have significantly reduced the time people spend in meetings compared to the meeting times before daily stand-ups became a way of work.

During the stand-ups, problems are not solved, but there is a routine in place to ensure they are rapidly resolved. If the problem requires collaboration with another squad member, it is noted, and those members will discuss it later in the day. If the problem requires IT-area lead support to resolve, the problem is noted and escalated. The IT-area lead may resolve it quickly, or take it to her/his stand-up to raise it with other IT-area leads or tribe leads to resolve. Once resolved, that information is rapidly relayed back through the channel. The problem remains visualized until it is resolved. Similarly, if the problem is technical in nature, it will be shared with the appropriate chapter or center of expertise. This pattern of vertical and horizontal communication is a leadership standard work practice called "catchball" (see Figure 16.3).

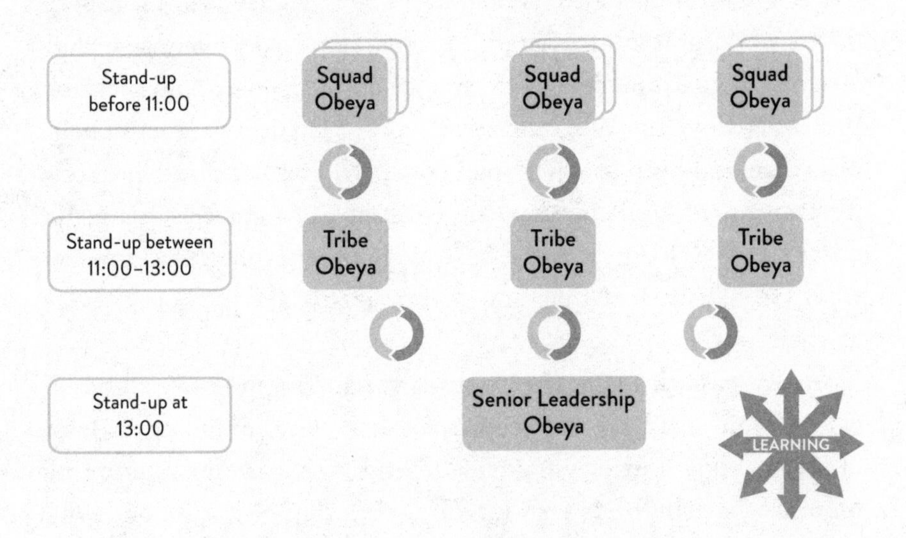

Figure 16.3: Stand-up and Catchball Rhythm

Using the same communication framework, other relevant learning is also relayed among squads, chapters, centers of expertise, and tribes, creating a natural vertical and horizontal flow of learning across all dimensions of the organization. This enables the squads to self-determine how best to craft their work to support overall enterprise strategy and enables effective prioritization. The tribe lead, in this case Jannes, also learns from the squad and chapter members, including lessons learned in their direct interaction with customers. This enables him to adapt his strategic thinking and goals and share insights with his peers and superiors.

This practice of rapid exchange of learning, enabling the frontline teams to learn about strategic priorities and the leaders to learn about customer experience from frontline team customer interaction, is a form of strategy deployment (Lean practitioners use the term Hoshin Kanri). It creates, at all levels, a continuous, rapid feedback cycle of learning, testing, validating, and adjusting, also known as PDCA.

In addition to regular stand-ups with squads, product owners, IT-area leads, and chapter leads, the tribe lead also regularly visits the squads to ask questions—not the traditional questions like "Why isn't this getting done?" but, rather, "Help me better understand the problems you're encountering," "Help me see what you're learning," and "What can I do to better support you and the team?" This kind of coaching behavior does not come easily to some leaders and managers. It takes real effort, with coaching, mentoring, and modeling (mentoring is being piloted within the Omnichannel Tribe, with plans for expansion) to change behavior from the traditional command-and-control to leaders-as-coaches where everyone's job is to (1) do the work, (2) improve the work, and (3) develop the people. The third objective—develop the people—is especially important in a technology domain, where automation is disrupting many technology jobs. For people to bring their best to the work that may, in fact, eliminate their current job, they need complete faith that their leaders value them—not just for their present work but for their ability to improve and innovate in their work. The work itself will constantly change; the organization that leads is the one with the people with consistent behavior to rapidly learn and adapt.

Not far from that squad space in a glass-enclosed meeting space with whiteboard-covered walls, a telepresence monitor, easel pads, and colorful, comfy chairs, we visit with Jordi de Vos, a young engineer whose entire career has been under Jannes' new way-of-working. Jordi is a chapter lead who also leads the effort toward one of the way-of-work strategic improvement objectives (recall that there are strategic improvement, performance monitoring, and portfolio roadmap strategic objectives). Jordi shares with others what he's learning about team security—the psychological safety for individuals to openly discuss problems and obstacles with no fear of harm or reprisal. He talks about this and other research he's discovering, how he's experimenting to learn what will resonate most among the squads, and what measurable changes are created and sustained. A fixed percentage of each squad's and chapter's time is allocated for improvement. Jordi says that the squads think of improvement activities as just regular work.

We ask Jordi what it's like to work within this culture. He reflects for a moment then shares a story. Jannes' tribes had been challenged by senior leadership to be twice as effective. "There was a tough deadline and lots of pressure. Our tribe lead, Jannes, went to the squads and said, 'If the quality isn't there, don't release. I'll cover your back.' So, we felt we owned quality. That helped us to do the right things."

Too often, quality is overshadowed by the pressure for speed. A courageous and supportive leader is crucial to help teams "slow down to speed up," providing them with the permission and safety to put quality first (fit for use and purpose) which, in the long run, improves speed, consistency, and capacity while reducing cost, delays, and rework. Best of all, this improves customer satisfaction and trust.

After this visit, we walk past more squad workspaces and more glass-enclosed meeting spaces, each with the same elements but different in their colors, textures, and furnishings. Back in the Leadership Obeya, we meet up with the coaching team for a healthy lunch and reflect on the many positive changes we've seen since our last visit. They share reflections on their current challenges and some of the approaches they are experimenting with to continue to spread and grow a generative culture, focusing on "going deep before going wide." Nevertheless, the pressure is there to scale wide and fast. Right now, one of the coaching team members is focusing on supporting culture change in just a few countries outside the Netherlands. Given that ING operates in over 40 countries, the discipline to allow time and attention for learning, rather than go for large scale change, is remarkable.

Another challenge the coaches are experimenting with is dispersed teams. With recent restructuring, some squads now have members from more than one country, so the coaching team is experimenting with, and measuring, ways to maintain the same high level of collaboration and learning among cross-border squads (it's very hard to virtually share two pizzas).

Not surprisingly, several of the most senior leaders and several other tribe lead peers want their own Obeya. The coaching team is hoping to approach this slowly enough so that real learning can occur. Transformational, generative leadership extends well beyond what is on the Obeya walls and the rhythm and routine of how you talk about it. "As a leader, you have to look at your own behaviors before you ask others to change," says Jannes. He will be the first to tell you that he is still learning. And in that, we believe, lies the secret to his success.

After lunch we head to the C-suite where we see a few of the senior leaders' Obeyas beginning to take shape. We run into Danny Wijnand, a chief design engineer who worked under Jannes until he was promoted last year to lead his own tribe. Danny reflects on the spread of this new way of work, beyond Jannes' tribes and out into the C-suite and across the rest of ING. "You get impatient wanting to speed their learning but then you realize you went through this yourself, and it took time. Storytelling is important, but they have to have their own learning."

Back again on the tribe floor, we visit with Jan Rijkhoff, a chapter lead. We wanted to learn about his chapter's current approach to problem solving. Over the years, they have experimented with different problem-solving methods, including A3, Kata, Lean startup, and others, and finally settled on a blend of elements that they found helpful, creating their own approach. In our walk today, we have seen evidence of multiple problem-solving initiatives in flight and visualized on the walls.

Their approach is to gather the right people who have experience and insights into the problem to rigorously examine the current condition. This rigor pays off, as the team gains insights that increase the probability of identifying the root cause rather than just the symptoms. With this learning, they form a hypothesis about an approach to improvement, including how and what to measure to learn if the experiment produces the desired outcomes. If the experiment is a success, they make it part of the standard work, share the learning, and continue to monitor to ensure the improvement is sustained. They apply this problem-solving approach at all levels of the organization. Sometimes a problem at a senior-leader level is analyzed and broken down into smaller parts, cascading to the chapter or squad level, for front-line analysis and controlled experimentation, with the learning feeding back up. "This approach works," Paul tells us when we meet up again, "because it helps people to embrace change, letting people come up with their own ideas, which they can then test out."

Amidst this colorful, creative work environment, with a philosophy of "make it your own," the idea of standard work may seem to be antithetical, even counterproductive. After all, this is knowledge work. Consider the notion of process (the way something is done) and practice (doing something that requires knowledge and judgment). For example, Scrum rituals are process; the act of understanding customer needs and writing the code is practice. So, when teams have a standard way of work, whether that work is to release effective code or to conduct a team stand-up meeting, following that standard saves a lot of time and energy. At ING, standard work is established not by imitating a way of work that is prescribed in a book or used successfully by another company. Instead, a team within ING experiments with different approaches and agrees upon the one best way to do the work. That rhythm and routine is spread to all similar teams. As conditions change, the standard is reevaluated and improved.

We catch up with Jannes as he concludes his day with a visit to the Leadership Obeya—to add a few Post-It note updates and to see what updates have been made by others. We ask about his thoughts on the journey they've been on. "The beginning insight was that our teams were not learning and not improving," he shared. "We were not able to get them to a level where they would be a continuously learning team. I saw that they wrestled with problems and other teams had solutions, and we were not able to bring them together to learn. When we were not able to learn as management, we were not able to help the teams to learn. We had to learn ourselves to become a learning team. We [his management team] experienced our own learning, then we went to the teams to help them learn to become a learning team."

We then asked about his approach to culture change. "Before, I never discussed culture," he said. "It was a difficult topic and I did not know how to change it in a sustainable way. But I learned that when you change the way you work, you change the routines, you create a different culture."

"Senior management is very happy with us," he adds with a broad smile, obviously proud of the people in his tribes. "We give them speed with quality. Sometimes, we may take a little longer than some of the others to reach green, but once we achieve it, we tend to stay green, when a lot of the others go back to red."

TRANSFORMING YOUR LEADERSHIP, MANAGEMENT, AND TEAM PRACTICES

We are often asked by enterprise leaders: How do we change our culture?

We believe the better questions to ask are: How do we learn how to learn? How do *I* learn? How can I make it safe for others to learn? How can I learn from and with them? How do we, together, establish new behaviors and new ways of thinking that build new habits, that cultivate our new culture? And where do we start?

At ING Netherlands, they began with a leader who asked himself these questions. He then brought on good coaches, tasked with challenging every person (including himself) to question assumptions and try new behaviors. He gathered his management team, saying, “Let’s try this together. Even if it doesn’t work, we will learn something that will help us to be better. Will you join me in this and see what we can learn?”

Each quarter his management team would come together for new learning and, over the next months, put that learning into practice. What, at first, felt uncomfortable for everyone became a little easier and, finally, became a habit—something they just did, just in time for the next learning cycle. They stretched and, just when they felt comfortable, stretched again. All along, they would reflect together and adjust when needed.

We recall in one boot camp session early on we challenged the management team members to develop simple leader standard work routines: visual management, regular stand-ups, and consistent coaching for their team members—replacing the long meetings and fire-fighting behaviors they were accustomed to. To develop this new way of working, first they needed to understand how they currently spent their time. The skepticism and discomfort were obvious; nevertheless, for several weeks each of them recorded and measured how they spent their time each day. They shared what they learned with each other, and together developed new ways to work.

When we returned for the next boot camp three months later, Mark Nijssen, one of the managers, welcomed us by saying, “I’ll never go back to the old way of working again!” Not only was adoption of basic leader standard work successful in helping them improve their effectiveness, they also managed to achieve the goal of making 10% of their time available to work on what they choose.

This willingness to experiment with new ways of thinking and working has led ING to where they are today. But it’s important to recognize that there is no checklist or playbook. You can’t "implement" culture change. Implementation thinking (attempting to mimic another company's specific behavior and practices) is, by its very nature, counter to the essence of generative culture.

At the end of this chapter is a table representing many of the practices described in this virtual visit to ING. Those marked with an (*) are practices that research shows to correlate with high performance. It's our hope that future research will explore the full range of practices listed here. This table is not to be used as a checklist but rather as a distillation or general guidelines for developing your own behaviors and practices (see Figure 16.4).

As you have seen in our virtual visit to ING, a high-performance culture is far more than just the application of tools, the adoption of a set of interrelated practices, copying the behaviors of other successful organizations, or the implementation of a prescribed, expert-designed framework. It is the development, through experimentation and learning guided by evidence, of a new way of working together that is situationally and culturally appropriate to each organization.

As you begin your own path to creating a learning organization, it's important to adopt and maintain the right mindset. Below are some suggestions we offer, based on our own experiences in helping enterprises evolve toward a high-performing, generative culture:

- Develop and maintain the right mindset. This is about learning and how to create an environment for shared organizational learning—not about just doing the practices, and certainly not about employing tools.
- Make it your own. This means three things:
  - Don't look to copy other enterprises on their methods and practices, or to implement an expert-designed model. Study and learn from them, but then experiment and adapt to what works for you and your culture.

	Team Practices	Management Practices	Leadership Practices
Culture	*Foster generative culture	*Foster generative culture	*Foster generative culture
	*Build quality in, continuously measure and monitor	*Focus on quality, protect teams to ensure quality	*Focus on quality, protect teams to ensure quality
	Focus on promoting organizational learning	Focus on promoting organizational learning	Focus on promoting organizational learning
		*Provide teams with time for improvement and innovation	*Provide teams with time for improvement and innovation
Organizational Structure			*Align, measure, and manage to flow (matrixed, cross-functional value stream organization structure)
		Establish small, cross-functional, multiskilled teams; support bridging structures so teams can easily communicate and collaborate	Enable and support cross-skilling to reduce expert-dependent bottlenecks, and form communities of expertise
			Establish and support internal coaches and the appropriate infrastructure to scale and sustain them
Direct Learning and Alignment to Value	*Engage, learn from, and validate with customers (Gemba)	*Engage with and learn from customers and teams (Gemba)	*Engage with and learn from customers, teams, supply chain partners, and other stakeholders (Gemba)
	*Understand & visualize customer value, identify measurable targets for quality	*Understand & visualize customer value, identify measurable targets for quality	
	*Practice creativity as part of overall work	*Practice creativity as part of overall work, encourage team members to utilize this time to learn and innovate	*Budget for and allocate time for creativity (i.e., Google's 20% target)
Strategy Deployment	*Visualize team goals and targets, understand how these targets advance enterprise strategy	Help teams to set and visualize goals and targets, understand and communicate how these targets advance enterprise strategy (catchball)	Practice strategy deployment, visualize all goals and near-term targets, communicate this clearly to managers and help them set appropriate targets and initiatives
	*Actively monitor and visualize performance to goals/targets	*Actively monitor and visualize performance to goals/targets	*Actively monitor and visualize performance to goals/targets
			Eliminate unnecessary controls, invest instead in process quality and team autonomy and capability (*teams that reported no approval process or used peer review achieved higher software delivery performance)
Improve Flow Through Analysis and Disciplined Problem Solving	Visualize & analyze workflow, identify obstacles to flow, (process/value stream mapping & analysis); *understand the connection between the work they do and its positive impact on customers	Visualize and analyze workflow, identify obstacles to flow, (process/value stream mapping & analysis), help teams understand how they support larger value stream	Visualize and analyze overall value stream flows (enterprise architecture), identify systemic obstacles to flow, prioritize and support mapping and analysis of lower-level supporting flows
	Prioritize obstacles to customer value and experience, and team targets and goals	Prioritize obstacles to customer value and experience, and team targets and goals	Prioritize systemic obstacles to flow
	Apply disciplined problem solving to prioritized problems, analyze to identify root causes	Apply disciplined problem solving to prioritized problems, analyze to identify root causes	Apply disciplined problem solving to complex systemic issues to identify strategic improvement themes and targets (strategy deployment), apply learning to update standard work
	Escalate cross-functional and systemic problems	Coordinate cross-functional problem solving, solve or escalate systemic problems	Cascade prioritized problem solving targets to the appropriate stakeholders through catchball PDCA
	Form hypotheses about root causes, design and conduct controlled experiments, measure results, communicate learnings, repeat if needed, incorporate improvements	Form hypotheses about root causes, design and conduct controlled experiments, measure results, communicate learnings, repeat if needed, incorporate improvements	Learn from organization-wide PDCA cycles, and repeat learning/improvement cycles
Way of Work, Rhythm, & Routine	*Visualize, measure, and monitor workflow, monitor for deviations, respond to deviations appropriately	*Visualize, measure, and monitor workflow, monitor for deviations, respond to deviations appropriately	*Visualize, measure, and monitor workflow, monitor for deviations, respond to deviations appropriately
	*Break demand into small elements (MVP's) and release regularly and often		
	*Visualize demand, WIP, and "done" (kanban)	*Visualize demand, WIP, and "done" (kanban)	*Visualize demand, WIP, and "done" (kanban)
	*Minimize and visualize WIP	*Minimize and visualize WIP	*Minimize and visualize WIP
	Prioritize demand to goals and targets	Prioritize demand to goals and targets	Prioritize demand to goals and targets
	Develop & practice team standard work (rhythm & routine)	Develop & practice leader standard work (rhythm & routine)	Develop & practice leader standard work (rhythm & routine)
	Conduct daily stand-ups with standard routine, escalate obstacles as needed (catchball)	Conduct daily stand-ups with team leads, standard routine, resolve or bridge/escalate obstacles as needed (catchball)	Conduct stand-ups with direct reports with standard routine on a regular cadence, resolve escalated obstacles (catchball)
	Support team and peer learning	Coach team members; support team learning	Coach managers, have your own coach
	Conduct regular cadence of retrospectives (work and way of work)	Conduct regular cadence of retrospectives (work and way of work)	Conduct regular cadence of retrospectives (work and way of work)

Figure 16.4: High-Performance Team, Management, and Leadership Behaviors and Practices (not a complete list, for a larger, downloadable version visit https://bit.ly/high-perf-behaviors-practices)

- Don't contract it out to a large consulting firm to expediently transform your organization or to implement new methodologies or practices for you. Your teams will feel that these methodologies (Lean, Agile, whatever) are being done *to* them. While your current processes may temporarily improve, your teams will not develop the confidence or capability to sustain, continue to improve, or to adapt and develop new processes and behaviors on their own.
- Do develop your own coaches. Initially you may need to hire outside coaching to establish a solid foundation, but you must ultimately be the agent of your own change. Coaching depth is a key lever for sustaining and scaling.

• You, too, need to change your way of work. Whether you are a senior leader, manager, or team member, lead by example. A generative culture starts with demonstrating new behaviors, not delegating them.
• Practice discipline. It was not easy for Jannes' management team to record and reflect on how they spent their time or try new things they weren't initially comfortable with in front of the people who reported to them. Change takes discipline and courage.
• Practice patience. Your current way of work took decades to entrench. It's going to take time to change actions and thought patterns until they become new habits and, eventually, your new culture.
• Practice practice. You just have to try it: learn, succeed, fail, learn, adjust, repeat. Rhythm and routine, rhythm and routine, rhythm and routine . . .

As you learn a new way of leading and working, you, and those you bring along with you on this journey, will explore, stretch, make some mistakes, get a lot right, learn, grow, and keep on learning. You'll discover better and faster ways to engage, learn, and adapt to changing conditions. In doing so, you'll improve quality and speed in everything you do. You'll grow your own leaders, innovate, and outperform your competition. You'll more rapidly and effectively improve value for customers and the enterprise. As the research shows, you'll "have a measurable impact on an organization's profitability, productivity, and market share. These also have an impact on customer satisfaction, efficiency, and the ability to achieve organizational goals."

We wish you all the best on your learning journey!

Steve and Karen

CONCLUSION

Over the past several years of surveying technology professionals and writing the State of DevOps Reports with the team at Puppet, we have discovered a lot about what makes high-performing teams and organizations. This journey has included researching technology transformations, publishing our results in peer review, and working with our colleagues and peers who are assessing and transforming their own organizations. Throughout this journey, we have made many breakthrough discoveries about the relationships between delivery performance, technical practices, cultural norms, and organizational performance.

In all of our research, one thing has proved consistently true: since nearly every company relies on software, delivery performance is critical to any organization doing business today. And software delivery performance is affected by many factors, including leadership, tools, automation, and a culture of continuous learning and improvement.

This book is a compilation of the things we found along that journey. In Part I, we presented what we found in our research. It starts with a discussion of why software delivery performance matters and how it drives organizational performance measures like profitability, productivity, and market share, as well as non-commercial measures like efficiency, effectiveness, customer satisfaction, and achieving mission goals. In this way, the ability to deliver quality software at high tempo with stability is a key value driver and differentiator for all organizations, regardless of size or industry vertical.

In Part II, we summarized the science behind the research and shed some light on the design decisions we made as well as the analysis methods we used. This provides the basis for the results we discuss in the bulk of the text.

We also identified the key capabilities that contribute to software delivery performance in statistically significant and meaningful ways. We hope that a discussion of what these practices are, with examples, will help you improve your own performance.

In Part III, we close with a discussion of organizational change management. To present this material, we reached out to colleagues Steve Bell and Karen Whitley Bell. Their contributed chapter presents one view of what following the capabilities and practices outlined in this book looks like and what it can provide for innovative organizations. You can begin your own technology transformation with everything we have learned in our research—transformation that so many others have been able to implement with great success in their own teams and organizations.

We hope this book has helped you identify areas where you can improve your own technology and business processes, work culture, and improvement cycles. Remember: you can't buy or copy high performance. You will need to develop your own capabilities as you pursue a path that fits your particular context and goals. This will take sustained effort, investment, focus, and time. However, our research is unequivocal. The results are worth it. We wish you all the best on your journey of improvement and look forward to hearing your stories.

APPENDIX A

CAPABILITIES TO DRIVE IMPROVEMENT

Our research has uncovered 24 key capabilities that drive improvements in software delivery performance in a statistically significant way. Our book details these findings. This appendix provides you with a handy list of these capabilities, each with a pointer to the chapter that covers it in detail (see also Figure A.1).

We have classified these capabilities into five categories:

- Continuous delivery
- Architecture
- Product and process
- Lean management and monitoring
- Cultural

Within each category, the capabilities are presented in no particular order.

CONTINUOUS DELIVERY CAPABILITIES

1. **Use version control for all production artifacts.** Version control is the use of a version control system, such as GitHub or Subversion, for all production artifacts,

including application code, application configurations, system configurations, and scripts for automating build and configuration of the environment. See Chapter 4.

2. **Automate your deployment process.** Deployment automation is the degree to which deployments are fully automated and do not require manual intervention. See Chapter 4.
3. **Implement continuous integration.** Continuous integration (CI) is the first step towards continuous delivery. This is a development practice where code is regularly checked in, and each check-in triggers a set of quick tests to discover serious regressions, which developers fix immediately. The CI process creates canonical builds and packages that are ultimately deployed and released. See Chapter 4.
4. **Use trunk-based development methods.** Trunk-based development has been shown to be a predictor of high performance in software development and delivery. It is characterized by fewer than three active branches in a code repository; branches and forks having very short lifetimes (e.g., less than a day) before being merged into master; and application teams rarely or never having "code lock" periods when no one can check in code or do pull requests due to merging conflicts, code freezes, or stabilization phases. See Chapter 4.
5. **Implement test automation.** Test automation is a practice where software tests are run automatically (not manually) continuously throughout the development process. Effective test suites are reliable—that is, tests

find real failures and only pass releasable code. Note that developers should be primarily responsible for creation and maintenance of automated test suites. See Chapter 4.

6. **Support test data management.** Test data requires careful maintenance, and test data management is becoming an increasingly important part of automated testing. Effective practices include having adequate data to run your test suite, the ability to acquire necessary data on demand, the ability to condition your test data in your pipeline, and the data not limiting the amount of tests you can run. We do caution, however, that teams should minimize, whenever possible, the amount of test data needed to run automated tests. See Chapter 4.
7. **Shift left on security.** Integrating security into the design and testing phases of the software development process is key to driving IT performance. This includes conducting security reviews of applications, including the infosec team in the design and demo process for applications, using preapproved security libraries and packages, and testing security features as a part of the automated testing suite. See Chapter 4.
8. **Implement continuous delivery (CD).** CD is a development practice where software is in a deployable state throughout its lifecycle, and the team prioritizes keeping the software in a deployable state over working on new features. Fast feedback on the quality and deployability of the system is available to all team members, and when they get reports that the system isn't deployable, fixes are made quickly. Finally, the system can be deployed to production or end users at any time, on demand. See Chapter 4.

ARCHITECTURE CAPABILITIES

9. **Use a loosely coupled architecture.** This affects the extent to which a team can test and deploy their applications on demand, without requiring orchestration with other services. Having a loosely coupled architecture allows your teams to work independently, without relying on other teams for support and services, which in turn enables them to work quickly and deliver value to the organization. See Chapter 5.
10. **Architect for empowered teams.** Our research shows that teams that can choose which tools to use do better at continuous delivery and, in turn, drive better software development and delivery performance. No one knows better than practitioners what they need to be effective. See Chapter 5. (The product management counterpart to this is found in Chapter 8.)

PRODUCT AND PROCESS CAPABILITIES

11. **Gather and implement customer feedback.** Our research has found that whether organizations actively and regularly seek customer feedback and incorporate this feedback into the design of their products is important to software delivery performance. See Chapter 8.
12. **Make the flow of work visible through the value stream.** Teams should have a good understanding of and visibility into the flow of work from the business all the way through to customers, including the status of products and features. Our research has found this has a positive impact on IT performance. See Chapter 8.

13. **Work in small batches.** Teams should slice work into small pieces that can be completed in a week or less. The key is to have work decomposed into small features that allow for rapid development, instead of developing complex features on branches and releasing them infrequently. This idea can be applied at the feature and the product level. (An MVP is a prototype of a product with just enough features to enable validated learning about the product and its business model.) Working in small batches enables short lead times and faster feedback loops. See Chapter 8.
14. **Foster and enable team experimentation.** Team experimentation is the ability of developers to try out new ideas and create and update specifications during the development process, without requiring approval from outside of the team, which allows them to innovate quickly and create value. This is particularly impactful when combined with working in small batches, incorporating customer feedback, and making the flow of work visible. See Chapter 8. (The technical counterpart to this is found in Chapter 4.)

LEAN MANAGEMENT AND MONITORING CAPABILITIES

15. **Have a lightweight change approval processes.** Our research shows that a lightweight change approval process based on peer review (pair programming or intrateam code review) produces superior IT performance than using external change approval boards (CABs). See Chapter 7.

16. **Monitor across application and infrastructure to inform business decisions.** Use data from application and infrastructure monitoring tools to take action and make business decisions. This goes beyond paging people when things go wrong. See Chapter 7.
17. **Check system health proactively.** Monitor system health, using threshold and rate-of-change warnings, to enable teams to preemptively detect and mitigate problems. See Chapter 13.
18. **Improve processes and manage work with work-in-process (WIP) limits.** The use of work-in-process limits to manage the flow of work is well known in the Lean community. When used effectively, this drives process improvement, increases throughput, and makes constraints visible in the system. See Chapter 7.
19. **Visualize work to monitor quality and communicate throughout the team.** Visual displays, such as dashboards or internal websites, used to monitor quality and work in process have been shown to contribute to software delivery performance. See Chapter 7.

CULTURAL CAPABILITIES

20. **Support a generative culture (as outlined by Westrum).** This measure of organizational culture is based on a typology developed by Ron Westrum, a sociologist who studied safety-critical complex systems in the domains of aviation and healthcare. Our research has found that this measure of culture is predictive of IT performance, organizational performance, and decreasing

burnout. Hallmarks of this measure include good information flow, high cooperation and trust, bridging between teams, and conscious inquiry. See Chapter 3.

21. **Encourage and support learning.** Is learning, in your culture, considered essential for continued progress? Is learning thought of as a cost or an investment? This is a measure of an organization's learning culture. See Chapter 10.
22. **Support and facilitate collaboration among teams.** This reflects how well teams, which have traditionally been siloed, interact in development, operations, and information security. See Chapters 3 and 5.
23. **Provide resources and tools that make work meaningful.** This particular measure of job satisfaction is about doing work that is challenging and meaningful, and being empowered to exercise your skills and judgment. It is also about being given the tools and resources needed to do your job well. See Chapter 10.
24. **Support or embody transformational leadership.** Transformational leadership supports and amplifies the technical and process work that is so essential in DevOps. It is comprised of five factors: vision, intellectual stimulation, inspirational communication, supportive leadership, and personal recognition. See Chapter 11.

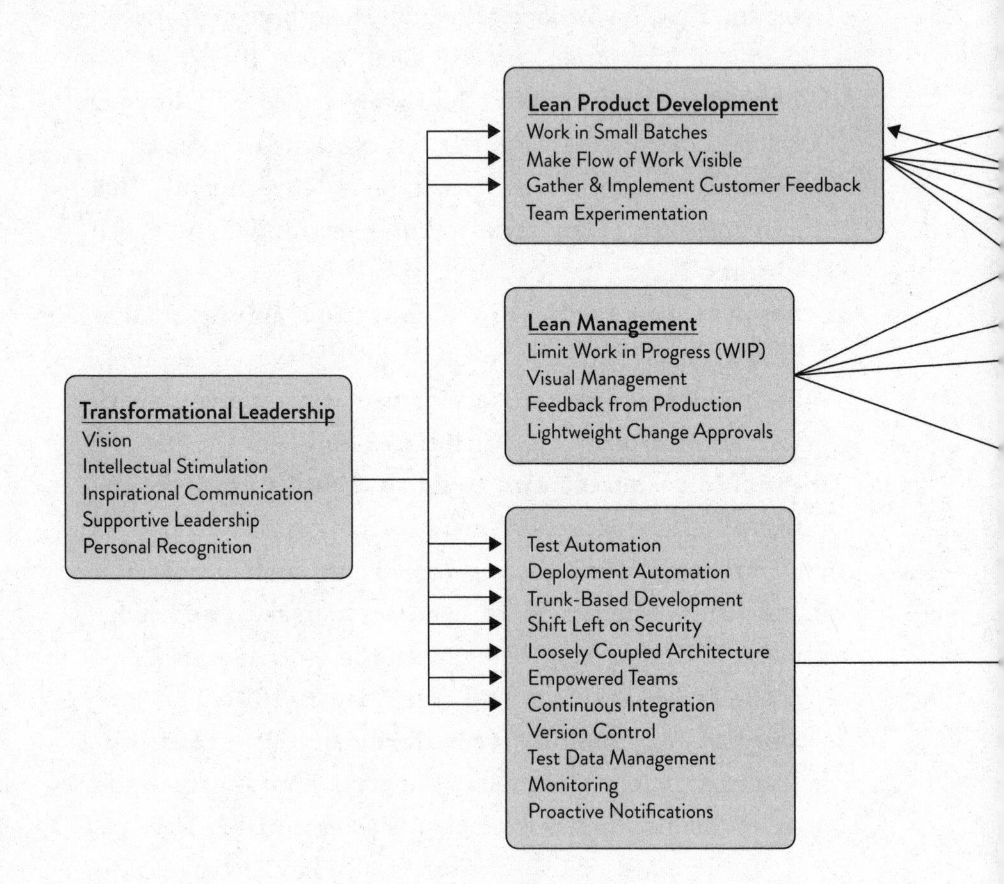

Figure A.1: Overall Research Program
(for a larger, downloadable version visit https://bit.ly/high-perf-behaviors-practices)

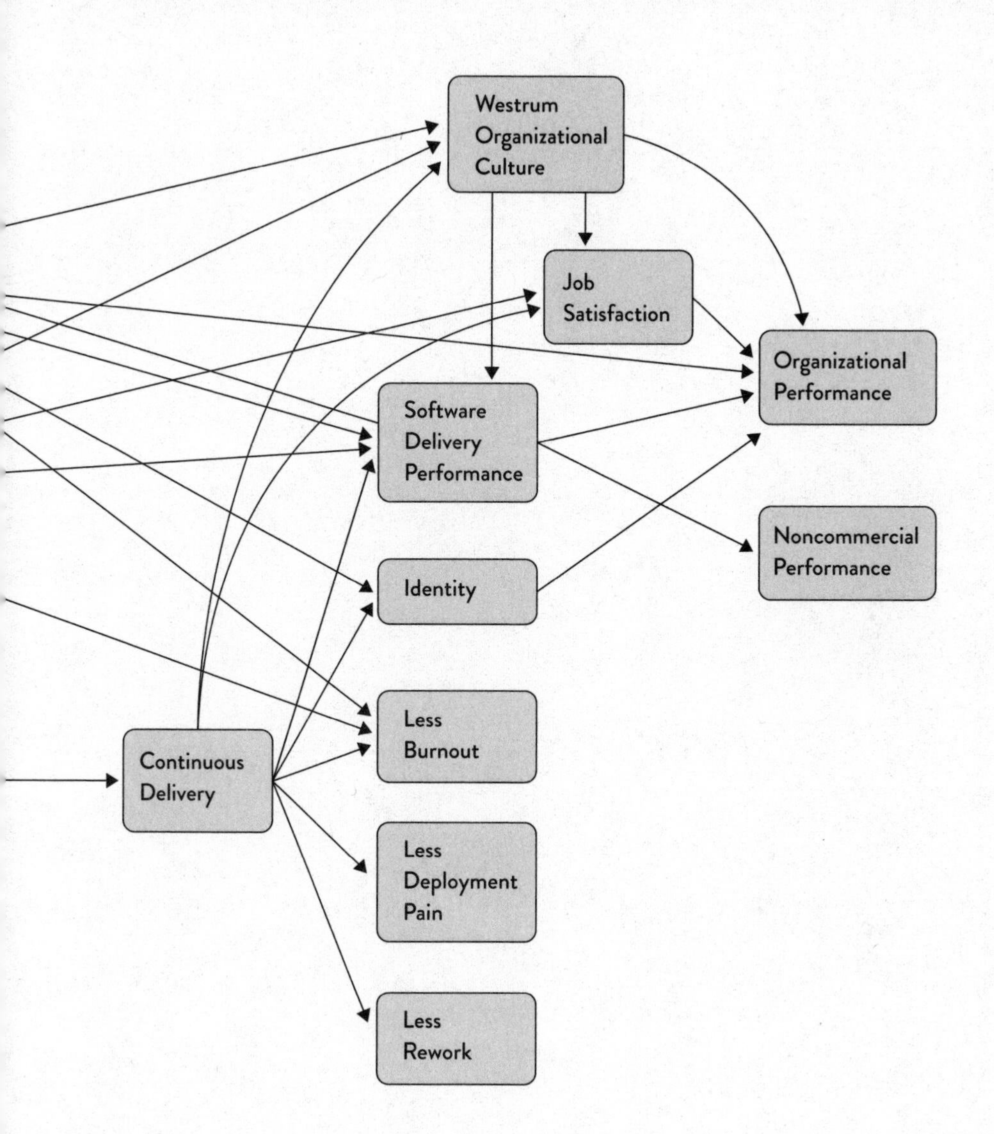
Westrum Organizational Culture
Job Satisfaction
Organizational Performance
Software Delivery Performance
Noncommercial Performance
Identity
Less Burnout
Continuous Delivery
Less Deployment Pain
Less Rework

APPENDIX B

THE STATS

Want to know what we've found from a statistical standpoint? Here is one place that lists it all, organized by category.

As a reminder:

Correlation looks at how closely two variables move together (or don't) but it doesn't tell us if one variable's movement predicts or causes the movement in another variable. Two variables moving together can always be due to a third variable or, sometimes, just chance.

Prediction talks about the impact of one construct on another. Specifically, we used inferential prediction, one of the most common types of analysis conducted in business and technology research today. It helps us understand the impact of HR policies, organizational behavior, and motivation, and helps us measure how technology affects such outcomes as user satisfaction, team efficiency, and organizational performance. Inferential design is used when purely experimental design is not possible and field experiments are preferred—for example, in business, where data collection happens in complex organizations, not in sterile lab environments, and companies won't sacrifice profits to fit into control groups defined by the research team. Analysis methods used to test prediction include simple linear regression and partial least squares regression, described in Appendix C.

ORGANIZATIONAL PERFORMANCE

- High performers are twice as likely to exceed organizational performance goals as low performers: profitability, productivity, market share, number of customers.
- High performers are twice as likely to exceed noncommercial performance goals as low performers: quantity of products/services, operating efficiency, customer satisfaction, quality of products/services, achieving organizational/mission goals.
- In a follow-up survey to the initial 2014 data collection effort, we gathered stock ticker data and performed additional analysis on responses from just over 1,000 respondents across 355 companies who volunteered the organization they worked for. For those who worked for publicly traded companies, we found the following (this analysis was not replicated in later years because our dataset was not large enough):
  - High performers had 50% higher market capitalization growth over three years compared to low performers.

SOFTWARE DELIVERY PERFORMANCE

- The four measures of software delivery performance (deploy frequency, lead time, mean time to restore, change fail percentage) are good classifiers for the software delivery performance profile. The groups we identified—high, medium, and low performers—are all significantly different across all four measures each year.

- Our analysis of high, medium, and low performers provides evidence that there are no trade-offs between improving performance and achieving higher levels of tempo and stability: they move in tandem.
- Software delivery performance predicts organizational performance and noncommercial performance.
- The software delivery performance construct is a combination of three metrics: lead time, release frequency, and MTTR. Change fail rate is not included in the construct, though it is highly correlated with the construct.
- Deploy frequency is highly correlated with continuous delivery and the comprehensive use of version control.
- Lead time is highly correlated with version control and automated testing.
- MTTR is highly correlated with version control and monitoring.
- Software delivery performance is correlated with organizational investment in DevOps.
- Software delivery performance is negatively correlated with deployment pain. The more painful code deployments are, the poorer the software delivery performance and culture.

QUALITY

- Unplanned work and rework:
  - High performers reported spending 49% of their time on new work and 21% on unplanned work or rework.
  - Low performers spend 38% of their time on new work and 27% on unplanned work or rework.

    - There is evidence of the J-curve in our rework data. Medium performers spend more time on unplanned rework than low performers, with 32% of their time spent on unplanned work or rework.
- Manual work:
    - High performers report the lowest amount of manual work across all practices (configuration management, testing, deployments, change approval process) at statistically significant levels.
    - There is evidence of the J-curve again. Medium performers do more manual work than low performers when it comes to deployment and change approval processes, and these differences are statistically significant.
    - See Table B.1 for manual work percentages in high, medium, and low performers.

Table B.1 Manual Work Percentages

Manual Work	High Performers	Medium Performers	Low Performers
Configuration management	28%	47%*	46%*
Testing	35%	51%*	49%*
Deployments	26%	47%	43%
Change approval process	48%	67%	59%

* Differences are not statistically significant between medium and low performers for configuration management and testing.

BURNOUT AND DEPLOYMENT PAIN

- Deployment pain is negatively correlated with software delivery performance and Westrum organizational culture.
- The five factors most highly correlated with burnout are Westrum organizational culture (negative), leaders (negative), organizational investment (negative), organizational performance (negative), and deployment pain (positive).

TECHNICAL CAPABILITIES

(Architecture capabilities are in their own section, below.)

- Trunk-based development:
  - High performers have the shortest integration times and branch lifetimes, with branch life and integration typically lasting hours or a day.
  - Low performers have the longest integration times and branch lifetimes, with branch life and integration typically lasting days or weeks.
- Technical practices predict continuous delivery, Westrum organizational culture, identity, job satisfaction, software delivery performance, less burnout, less deployment pain, and less time spent on rework.
- High performers spend 50% less time remediating security issues than low performers.

ARCHITECTURE CAPABILITIES

- There was no correlation between a particular type of system (e.g., system of engagement or system of record) and software delivery performance.
- Low performers were more likely to say that the software they were building—or the set of services they had to interact with—was "custom software developed by another company (e.g., an outsourcing partner)."
- Low performers were more likely to be working on mainframe systems.
- Having to integrate against mainframe systems was not a statistically significant indicator of performance.
- Medium and high performers have no significant correlation between system type and software delivery performance.
- A loosely coupled, well-encapsulated architecture drives IT performance. In the 2017 dataset, this was the biggest contributor to continuous delivery.
- Among those who deploy at least once per day, as the number of developers on the team increases we found:
  - Low performers deploy with decreasing frequency.
  - Medium performers deploy at a constant frequency.
  - High performers deploy at a significantly increasing frequency.
- High-performing teams were more likely to respond positively to the following statements:
  - We can do most of our testing without requiring an integrated environment.
  - We can and do deploy/release our applications independently of other applications/services they depend on.

- It is custom software that uses a microservices architecture.

- We found no significant differences according to which type of architecture teams were building or integrating against.

LEAN MANAGEMENT CAPABILITIES

- Lean management capabilities predict Westrum organizational culture, job satisfaction, software delivery performance, and less burnout.
- Change approvals:
  - Change advisory boards are negatively correlated with software delivery performance.
  - Approval only for high-risk changes was not correlated with software delivery performance.
  - Teams that reported no approval process or used peer review achieved higher software delivery performance.
  - A lightweight change approval process predicts software delivery performance.

LEAN PRODUCT MANAGEMENT CAPABILITIES

- The ability to take an experimental approach to product development is highly correlated with the technical practices that contribute to continuous delivery.
- Lean product development capabilities predict Westrum organizational culture, software delivery performance, organizational performance, and less burnout.

ORGANIZATIONAL CULTURE CAPABILITIES

- These measures are strongly correlated to culture:
  - Organizational investment in DevOps
  - The experience and effectiveness of team leaders
  - Continuous delivery capabilities
  - The ability of development, operations, and infosec teams to achieve win-win outcomes
  - Organizational performance
  - Deployment pain
  - Lean management practices
- Westrum organizational culture predicts software delivery performance, organizational performance, and job satisfaction.
- Westrum organizational culture is negatively correlated with deployment pain. The more painful code deployments are, the poorer the culture.

IDENTITY, EMPLOYEE NET PROMOTER SCORE (ENPS), AND JOB SATISFACTION

- Identity predicts organizational performance.
- High performers have better employee loyalty, as measured by employee Net Promoter Score (eNPS). Employees in high-performing organizations were 2.2 times more likely to recommend their organization as a great place to work.
- eNPS was significantly correlated with:
  - The extent to which the organization collects customer feedback and uses it to inform the design of products and features

- The ability of teams to visualize and understand the flow of products or features through development all the way to the customer
- The extent to which employees identify with their organization's values and goals, and the effort they are willing to put in to make the organization successful

- Employees in high-performing teams are 2.2 times more likely to recommend their *organization* as a great place to work.
- Employees in high-performing teams are 1.8 times more likely to recommend their *team* as a great place to work.
- Job satisfaction predicts organizational performance.

LEADERSHIP

- We observed significant differences in leadership characteristics among high-, medium-, and low-performing teams.
  - High-performing teams reported having leaders with the strongest behaviors across all dimensions: vision, inspirational communication, intellectual stimulation, supportive leadership, and personal recognition.
  - Low-performing teams reported the lowest levels of all five leadership characteristics.
  - These differences were all at statistically significant levels.
- Characteristics of transformational leadership are highly correlated with software delivery performance.
- Transformational leadership is highly correlated with employee Net Promoter Score (eNPS).

- Teams with the top 10% of reported transformational leadership characteristics were equally or even less likely to be high performers, compared to the entire population of teams represented in survey results.
- Leadership is predictive of Lean product development capabilities (working in small batches, team experimentation, gathering and implementing customer feedback) and technical practices (test automation, deployment automation, trunk-based development, shift left on security, loosely coupled architecture, empowered teams, continuous integration).

DIVERSITY

- Of the total respondents, 5% self-identified as women in 2015, 6% in 2016, and 6.5% in 2017.
- 33% of our respondents report working on teams with no women.
- 56% of our respondents report working on teams that are less than 10% female.
- 81% of our respondents report working on teams that are less than 25% female.
- Gender
  - 91% Male
  - 6% Female
  - 3% Non-binary or other
- Underrepresented
  - 77% responded no, I do not identify as underrepresented.
  - 12% responded yes, I identify as underrepresented.
  - 11% responded that they preferred not to respond or NA.

OTHER

- Investment in DevOps was highly correlated to software delivery performance.
- Percentage of people reporting working in DevOps teams has grown over the last four years:
  - 16% in 2014
  - 19% in 2015
  - 22% in 2016
  - 27% in 2017
- DevOps is happening across all operating systems. We first started asking about this in 2015.
  - 78% of respondents are widely deployed on 1–4 different operating systems, the most popular being: Enterprise Linux, Windows 2012, Windows 2008, Debian/Ubuntu Linux.
- Figure B.1 shows the Firmographics from the 2017 data. We note that high, medium, and low performers see representation from all groups. That is, there are large enterprises in the high-, medium-, and low-performing groups. We also see startups in high-, medium-, and low-performing groups. Highly regulated industries (including financial, healthcare, telecommunications, etc.) are also found in the high-, medium-, and low-performing groups. What matters is not what industry you're in or how big you are; even large, highly regulated organizations are able to develop and deliver software with high performance, and then leverage these capabilities to deliver value to their customers and their organization.

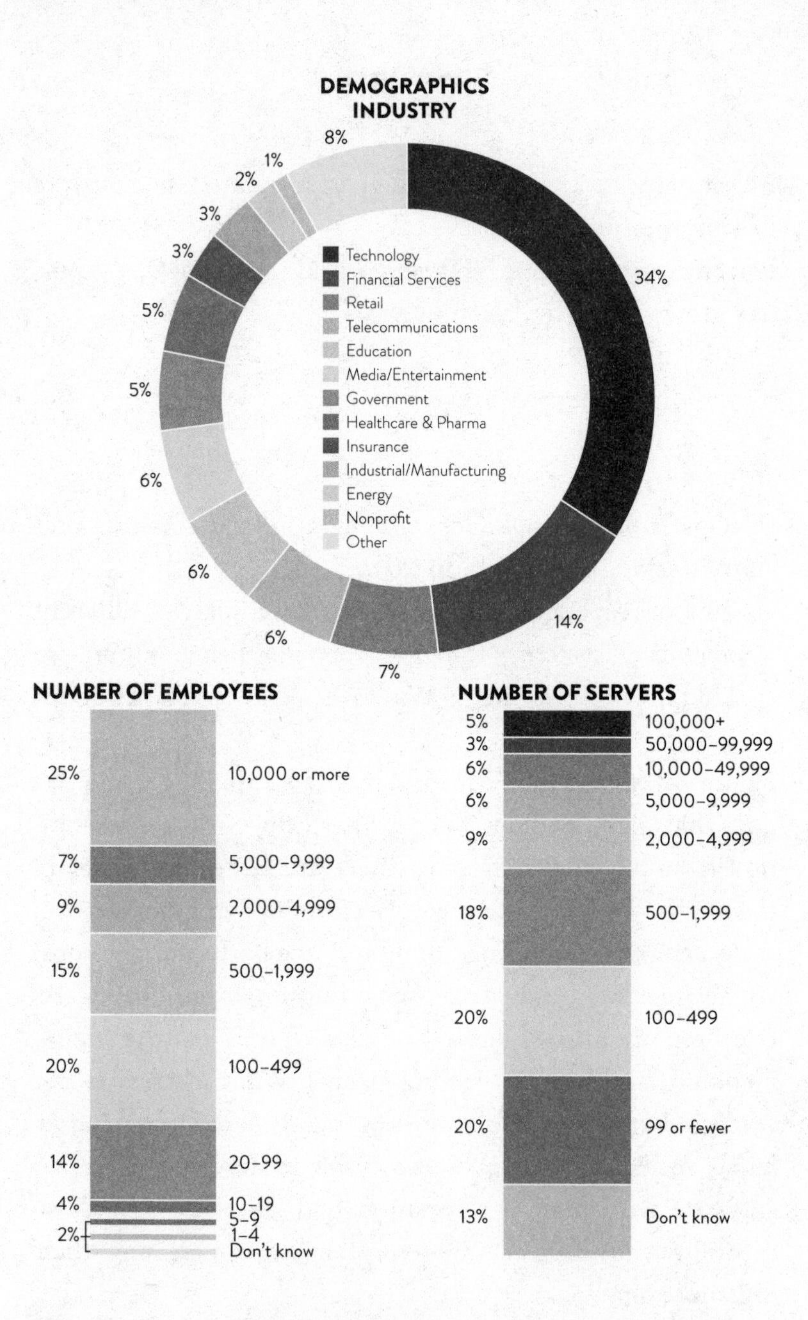

Figure B.1: Firmographics: Organization Size, Industry, Number of Servers in 2017

APPENDIX C

STATISTICAL METHODS USED IN OUR RESEARCH

This appendix is a brief summary of the statistical methods used in our research. It is meant to serve as a reference, not a detailed statistical text. We have included pointers to the relevant academic references where appropriate. The appendix roughly follows our path through research design and analysis.

SURVEY PREPARATION

Once we have decided on the constructs and hypotheses we want to test each year, we begin the research process by designing the survey instrument.[1]

When possible, previously validated items are used. Examples include organizational performance (Widener 2007) and non-commercial performance (Cavalluzzo and Ittner 2004). When we create our own measures, the survey instrument is developed following commonly accepted procedures adapted from Dillman (1978).

[1] We decide on our research model each year based on a review of the literature, a review of our previous research findings, and a healthy debate.

DATA COLLECTION

Armed with our research design and survey questions, we set out to collect data.

We collected data using snowball sampling, a nonprobabilistic technique. Details on why this is an appropriate technique, how we collected our sample, and strategies we used to counteract limitations of the technique are given in Chapter 15.

TESTS FOR BIAS

Once we have our data, we start by testing for bias.

- **Chi-square tests.** A test for differences. This is used to check for significant differences in variables that can only take on categorical values (for example, gender).
- **T-tests.** A test for differences. This is used to check for significant differences in variables that can take on scale values (for example, Likert values). We used this to check for differences between early and late responders.
- **Common method bias (CMB)** or **common method variance (CMV).** This involves conducting two tests:
  - **Harman's single-factor test** (Podsakoff and Dalton 1987). This checks to see if a single factor features significant loading for all items.
  - **The marker variable test** (Lindell and Whitney 2001). This checks to see if all originally significant correlations remain significant after adjusting for the second-lowest positive correlation among the constructs.

We did not see bias between early and late responders. Common-method bias does not seem to be a problem with our samples.

TESTING FOR RELATIONSHIPS

Consistent with best practices and accepted research, we conducted our analysis in two stages (Gefen and Straub 2005). In the first step, we conduct analyses on the measures to validate and form our latent constructs (see Chapter 13). This allows us to determine which constructs can be included in the second stage of our research.

TESTS OF THE MEASUREMENT MODEL

- **Principal components analysis (PCA).** A test to help confirm convergent validity. This method is used to help explain the variance-covariance structure of a set of variables.
  - Principal components analysis was conducted with varimax rotation, with separate analyses for independent and dependent variables (Straub et al. 2004).
  - There are two types of PCA that can be done: confirmatory factor analysis (CFA) and exploratory factor analysis (EFA). In almost all cases, we performed EFA. We chose this method because it is a stricter test used to uncover the underlying structure of the variables without imposing or suggesting a structure a priori. (One notable exception was when we used CFA to confirm the validity for transformational leadership; this was selected because

the items are well-established in the literature.) Items should load on their respective constructs higher than 0.60 and should not cross-load.

- **Average variance extracted (AVE).** A test to help confirm both convergent and discriminant validity. AVE is a measure of the amount of variance that is captured by a construct in relation to the amount of variance due to measurement error.
  - AVE must be greater than 0.50 to indicate convergent validity.
  - The square root of the AVE must be greater than any cross-diagonal correlations of the constructs (when you place the square root of the AVE on the diagonal of a correlation table) to indicate divergent validity.
- **Correlation.** This test helps confirm divergent validity when correlations between constructs are below 0.85 (Brown 2006). Pearson correlations were used (see below for details).
- **Reliability**
  - **Cronbach's alpha:** A measure of internal consistency. The acceptable cutoff for CR is 0.70 (Nunnally 1978); all constructs met either this cutoff or CR (listed next). Note that Cronbach's alpha is known to be biased against small scales (i.e., constructs with a low number of items), so both Cronbach's alpha and composite reliability were run to confirm reliability.
  - **Composite reliability (CR):** A measure of internal consistency and convergent validity. The acceptable cutoff for CR is 0.70 (Chin et al. 2003); all constructs either met this cutoff or Cronbach's alpha (listed above).

All of the above tests must pass for a construct to be considered suitable for use in further analysis. We say that a construct "exhibits good psychometric properties" if this is the case, and proceed. All constructs used in our research passed these tests.

TESTS FOR RELATIONSHIPS (CORRELATION AND PREDICTION) AND CLASSIFICATION

In the second step, we take the measures that have passed the first step of measurement validation and test our hypotheses. These are the statistical tests that are used in this phase of the research. As outlined in Chapter 12, in this research design we test for inferential prediction, which means all tested hypotheses are supported by additional theories and literature. If no supporting theories exist to suggest that a predictive relationship exists, we only report correlations.

- **Correlation.** Signifies a mutual relationship or connection between two or more constructs. We use Pearson correlation in this research, which is the correlation most often used in business contexts today. Pearson correlation measures the strength of a linear relationship between two variables, called Pearson's r. It is often referred to as just correlation and takes a value between –1 and 1. If two variables have a perfect linear correlation, i.e., move together exactly, $r = 1$. If they move in exactly opposite directions, $r = -1$. If they are not correlated at all, $r = 0$.

- **Regression.** This is used to test predictive relationships. There are several kinds of regression. We used two types of linear regression in this research, as described below.
  - **Partial least squares regression (PLS).** This was used to test predictive relationships in years 2015 through 2017. PLS is a correlation-based regression method that was selected for our analysis for a few reasons (Chin 2010):
    - This method optimizes for prediction of the outcome variable. As we wanted our results to be beneficial to the practitioners in the industry, this was important to us.
    - PLS does not require assumptions of multivariate normality. Said another way, this method doesn't require that our data be normally distributed.
    - PLS is a great choice for exploratory research—and that's exactly what our research program is!
  - **Linear regression.** This was used to test predictive relationships in our 2014 research.

TESTS FOR CLASSIFICATION

These tests could be done at any time, because they don't rely on constructs.

- **Cluster analysis.** This was used to develop a data-driven classification of software delivery performance, giving us high, medium, and low performers. In cluster analysis, each measurement is put on a separate dimension, and the clustering algorithm attempts to minimize the distance between all cluster members and maximize the distance among clusters. Cluster analysis was conducted using five methods: Ward's (1963), between-groups linkage, within-groups linkage, centroid, and median. The results for cluster solutions were compared in terms of: (a) change in fusion coefficients, (b) number of individuals in each cluster (solutions including clusters with few individuals were excluded), and (c) univariate F-statistics (Ulrich and McKelvey 1990). Based on these criteria, the solution using Ward's method performed best and was selected. We used the hierarchical cluster analysis method because:

- It has strong explanatory power (letting us understand parent-child relationships in the clusters).
- We did not have any industry or theoretical reasons to have a predetermined number of clusters. That is, we wanted the data to determine the number of clusters we should have.
- Our dataset was not too big. (Hierarchical clustering is not suitable for extremely large datasets.)

• **Analysis of variance (ANOVA).** To interpret the clusters, post hoc comparisons of the means of the software delivery performance outcomes (deploy frequency, lead time, MTTR, and change fail rate) were conducted using Tukey's test. Tukey's was selected because it does not require normality; Duncan's multiple range test was also run to test for significant differences and in all cases the results were the same (Hair et al. 2006). Pairwise comparisons were done across clusters using each software delivery performance variable, and significant differences sorted the clusters into groups wherein that variable's mean value does not significantly differ across clusters within a group, but differs at a statistically significant level ($p < 0.10$ in our research) across clusters in different groups. In all years except 2016 (see Chapter 2 callout for the Surprise), high performers saw the best performance on all variables, low performers saw the worst performance on all variables, and medium performers saw the middle performance on all variables—all at statistically significant levels.

ACKNOWLEDGMENTS

This book emerged from the partnership between DORA and Puppet on the State of DevOps Reports. Thus, we'd like to start by thanking the Puppet team, and in particular Alanna Brown and Nigel Kersten who were the principal contributors from the Puppet side. We'd also like to thank Aliza Earnshaw for her meticulous work editing the State of DevOps Reports over several years. The report would not be the same without her careful eye.

The authors would also like to thank several people who helped develop the hypotheses we test in the report. From 2016, we thank Steven Bell and Karen Whitley Bell for their promptings to investigate Lean product management, and for their time spent on research and discussions with the team on the theories of value stream and visibility of customer feedback. From 2017, we thank Neal Ford, Martin Fowler, and Mik Kersten for the items measuring architecture, and Amy Jo Kim and Mary Poppendieck for team experimentation.

Several experts kindly donated their time to help review early drafts of this book. We'd like to offer deep gratitude to Ryn Daniels, Jennifer Davis, Martin Fowler, Gary Gruver, Scott Hain, Dmitry Kirsanov, Courtney Kissler, Bridget Kromhout, Karen Martin, Dan North, and Tom Poppendieck.

We'd like to thank Anna Noak, Todd Sattersten, and the whole IT Revolution team for all their hard work on this project. Finally, Dmitry Kirsanov and Alina Kirsanova took care of copyediting, proofreading, indexing, and composing the book with distinctive thoroughness and care. Thank you.

NICOLE

First and foremost, many thanks to my coauthors and collaborators, without whom this work wouldn't be possible. Y'all didn't kick me off the project when I first showed up and told you it was wrong—politely, I hope. Jez, I've learned patience, empathy, and a renewed love for tech I thought had waned. Gene, your boundless enthusiasm and drive for "just one more analysis!" keeps our work strong and exciting. The data for this project comes from the State of DevOps Reports, which were conducted with Puppet Inc. From the Puppet team, Nigel Kersten and Alanna Brown: thank you for your collaboration and helping us to craft a narrative that resonates with our audience. And of course Aliza Earnshaw: your skill goes far beyond copyediting and made my work infinitely better. I loved that we could hash it out until we reached agreement; when you told me I was "meticulously rigorous," it was the best compliment ever.

A very special thank you goes to my dad for instilling in me a sense of curiosity, a need for excellence, and an inability to take sh*t from people who don't think I can do something. It has all come in handy over the years, particularly as a woman in tech. Sorry you missed the party, Dad. Many thanks to my mom for always being my #1 cheerleader and supporter; whatever my crazy plans, she always trusts me. I love you both.

As always, my biggest thanks and deepest gratitude go to Xavier Velasquez. My best friend and first sounding board, you've been there for the entire journey—when it was inspired from an odd usability study in the midst of a storm, to a hard pivot in my PhD program, then inviting myself into the State of DevOps Reports, and now finally this book. Your support, encouragement, and wisdom—in life and in tech—have been invaluable.

Suzie! How did I ever get so lucky? I had an advisor who took a gamble on a PhD student who promised you that studying tech professionals, their tools, and their environment—and how it all impacted their work—would be important and relevant. (Those at top PhD programs will understand that this is, indeed, a gamble, with real risks involved.) Ten years later, my research has grown and evolved and we call it DevOps. Many thanks to you, Suzanne Weisband, for trusting my instincts and guiding my research those early years. You've been the best advisor, cheerleader, and now friend.

To my post-doc advisors, mentors, and frequent peer-review coauthors Alexandra Durcikova and Rajiv Sabherwal: you also took risks conducting research with me in a new context, and I have learned so much from our collaborations. My methods are stronger, my arguments more reasoned, and my ability to see a problem space is more developed. Thank you.

Many thanks to the DevOps community, who welcomed and accepted a crazy researcher and have participated in the studies and shared your stories. My work is better because of you, and more importantly, I am better because of you. Much love.

And finally, thanks to Diet Coke for getting me through long stints of writing and editing.

JEZ

Many thanks to my wife and BFF Rani for supporting me working on this book even after I promised I wouldn't write another one. You're the best! I love you. Thanks to my daughters for bringing so much fun and joy into the proceedings, and to my mum and dad for supporting my adventures with computers as a kid.

Nicole took an industry survey, Puppet's State of DevOps Report, and turned it into a scientific tool. Our industry has always struggled with applying science to the development and operation of software products and services. The social systems that support software delivery are too irreducibly complex to make randomized, controlled experiments practical. In retrospect, the solution was clear: use behavioral science to study these systems. Nicole's careful, thorough pioneering of this approach has produced incredible results, and it's hard to overstate the impact of her work. It's been an honor to be her partner in this research, and I've learned an enormous amount. Thank you.

The reason I'm involved with this project at all is Gene, who invited me to be part of the State of DevOps team back in 2012. Gene, your passion for this project—and, on a personal level, for challenging my hypotheses and analysis (yes, I'm talking about trunk-based development)—has made this both substantially more rigorous and highly rewarding.

I also want to thank the Puppet team who've contributed so much to this work and without whom it wouldn't exist, particularly Alanna Brown, Nigel Kersten, and Aliza Earnshaw. Thank you.

GENE

I am grateful to Margueritte, my loving wife of twelve years, as well as my sons, Reid, Parker, and Grant—I know that I could not do the work I love without their support and tolerance of deadlines, late nights, and round-the-clock texting. And of course, my parents, Ben and Gail Kim, for helping me become a nerd early in life.

This research with Jez and Nicole has been some of the most satisfying and illuminating I've ever had the privilege of working on—no one could ask for a better team of collaborators. I genuinely believe this work significantly advances our profession, by helping us better define how we improve technology work, through rigorous theory building and testing.

And of course, thank you to Alanna Brown and Nigel Kersten at Puppet for the amazing 5+ year collaboration on State of DevOps project, from which so much of this book is based upon.

BIBLIOGRAPHY

ACMQueue. “Resilience Engineering: Learning to Embrace Failure.” *ACMQueue* 10, no. 9 (2012). http://queue.acm.org/detail.cfm?id=2371297.

Alloway, Tracy Packiam, and Ross G. Alloway. “Working Memory across the Lifespan: A Cross-Sectional Approach.” *Journal of Cognitive Psychology* 25, no. 1 (2013): 84–93.

Almeida, Thiago. https://www.devopsdays.org/events/2016-london/program/thiago-almeida/.

Azzarello, Domenico, Frédéric Debruyne, and Ludovica Mottura. “The Chemistry of Enthusiasm.” Bain.com. May 4, 2012. http://www.bain.com/publications/articles/the-chemistry-of-enthusiasm.aspx.

Bansal, Pratima. “From Issues to Actions: The Importance of Individual Concerns and Organizational Values in Responding to Natural Environmental Issues.” *Organization Science* 14, no. 5 (2003): 510–527.

Beck, Kent, et al. “Manifesto for Agile Software.” AgileManifesto.org. 2001. http://agilemanifesto.org/.

Behr, Kevin, Gene Kim, and George Spafford. *The Visible Ops Handbook: Starting ITIL in 4 Practical Steps*. Eugene, OR: Information Technology Process Institute, 2004.

Bessen, James E. *Automation and Jobs: When Technology Boosts Employment*. Boston University School of Law, Law and Economics Paper, no. 17–09 (2017).

Blank, Steve. *The Four Steps to the Epiphany: Successful Strategies for Products That Win*. BookBaby, 2013.

Bobak, M., Z. Skodova, and M. Marmot. “Beer and Obesity: A Cross-Sectional Study.” *European Journal of Clinical Nutrition* 57, no. 10 (2003): 1250–1253.

Brown, Timothy A. *Confirmatory Factor Analysis for Applied Research*. New York: Guilford Press, 2006.

Burton-Jones, Andrew, and Detmar Straub. “Reconceptualizing System Usage: An Approach and Empirical Test.” *Information Systems Research* 17, no. 3 (2006): 228–246.

Carr, Nicholas G. “IT Doesn’t Matter.” *Educause Review* 38 (2003): 24–38.

Cavalluzzo, K. S., and C. D. Ittner. "Implementing Performance Measurement Innovations: Evidence from Government." *Accounting, Organizations and Society* 29, no. 3 (2004): 243–267.

Chandola, T., E. Brunner, and M. Marmot. "Chronic Stress at Work and the Metabolic Syndrome: Prospective Study." *BMJ* 332, no. 7540 (2006): 521–525.

Chin, Wynne W. "How to Write Up and Report PLS Analyses." In: V. Esposito Vinzi, W. W. Chin, J. Henseler, and H. Wang (eds.), *Handbook of Partial Least Squares*. Berlin: Springer (2010): 655–690.

Chin, Wynne W., Barbara L. Marcolin, and Peter R. Newsted. "A Partial Least Squares Latent Variable Modeling Approach for Measuring Interaction Effects: Results from a Monte Carlo Simulation Study and an Electronic-Mail Emotion/Adoption Study." *Information Systems Research* 14, no. 2 (2003): 189–217.

Conway, Melvin E. "How Do Committees Invent?" *Datamation* 14, no. 5 (1968): 28–31.

Corman, Joshua, David Rice, and Jeff Williams. "The Rugged Manifesto." Rugged-Software.org. September 4, 2012. https://www.ruggedsoftware.org/.

Covert, Bryce. "Companies with Female CEOs Beat the Stock Market." ThinkProgress.org. July 8, 2014. https://thinkprogress.org/companies-with-female-ceos-beat-the-stock-market-2d1da9b3790a.

Covert, Bryce. "Returns for Women Hedge Fund Managers Beat Everyone Else's." ThinkProgress.org. January 15, 2014. https://thinkprogress.org/returns-for-women-hedge-fund-managers-beat-everyone-elses-a4da2d7c4032.

Deloitte. *Waiter, Is That Inclusion in My Soup?: A New Recipe to Improve Business Performance.* Sydney, Australia: Deloitte, 2013.

Diaz, Von, and Jamilah King. "How Tech Stays White." Colorlines.com. October 22, 2013. http://www.colorlines.com/articles/how-tech-stays-white.

Dillman, D. A. *Mail and Telephone Surveys*. New York: John Wiley & Sons, 1978.

Deming, W. Edwards. *Out of the Crisis*. Cambridge, MA: MIT Press, 2000.

East, Robert, Kathy Hammond, and Wendy Lomax. "Measuring the Impact of Positive and Negative Word of Mouth on Brand Purchase Probability." *International Journal of Research in Marketing* 25, no. 3 (2008): 215–224.

Elliot, Stephen. *DevOps and the Cost of Downtime: Fortune 1000 Best Practice Metrics Quantified.* Framingham, MA: International Data Corporation, 2014.

Foote, Brian, and Joseph Yoder. "Big Ball of Mud." *Pattern Languages of Program Design* 4 (1997): 654–692.

Forsgren, Nicole, Alexandra Durcikova, Paul F. Clay, and Xuequn Wang. "The Integrated User Satisfaction Model: Assessing Information Quality and System Quality as Second-Order Constructs in System Administration." *Communications of the Association for Information Systems* 38 (2016): 803–839.

Forsgren, Nicole, and Jez Humble. "DevOps: Profiles in ITSM Performance and Contributing Factors." At the *Proceedings of the Western Decision Sciences Institute (WDSI) 2016*, Las Vegas, 2016.

Gartner. *Gartner Predicts*. 2016. http://www.gartner.com/binaries/content/assets/events/keywords/infrastructure-operations-management/iome5/gartner-predicts-for-it-infrastructure-and-operations.pdf.

Gefen, D., and D. Straub. "A Practical Guide to Factorial Validity Using PLS-Graph: Tutorial and Annotated Example." *Communications of the Association for Information Systems* 16, art. 5 (2005): 91–109.

Goh, J., J. Pfeffer, S. A. Zenios, and S. Rajpal. "Workplace Stressors & Health Outcomes: Health Policy for the Workplace." *Behavioral Science & Policy* 1, no. 1 (2015): 43–52.

Google. "The Five Keys to a Successful Google Team." ReWork blog. November 17, 2015. https://rework.withgoogle.com/blog/five-keys-to-a-successful-google-team/.

Hair, J. F., W. C. Black, B. J. Babin, R. E. Anderson, and R. L. Tatham. *Multivariate Data Analysis*, 2nd ed. Upper Saddle River, NJ: Pearson Prentice Hall, 2006.

Humble, Jez. "Cloud Infrastructure in the Federal Government: Modern Practices for Effective Risk Management." Nava Public Benefit Corporation, 2017. https://devops-research.com/assets/federal-cloud-infrastructure.pdf.

Humble, Jez, and David Farley. *Continuous Delivery: Reliable Software Releases through Build, Test, and Deployment Automation*. Upper Saddle River, NJ: Addison-Wesley, 2010.

Humble, Jez, Joanne Molesky, and Barry O'Reilly. *Lean Enterprise: How High Performance Organizations Innovate at Scale*. Sebastopol, CA: O'Reilly Media, 2014.

Hunt, Vivian, Dennis Layton, and Sara Prince. "Why Diversity Matters." McKinsey.com. January 2015. https://www.mckinsey.com/business-functions/organization/our-insights/why-diversity-matters.

Johnson, Jeffrey V., and Ellen M. Hall. "Job Strain, Work Place Social Support, and Cardiovascular Disease: A Cross-Sectional Study of a Random Sample of the Swedish Working Population." *American Journal of Public Health* 78, no. 10 (1988): 1336–1342.

Kahneman, D. *Thinking, Fast and Slow*. New York: Macmillan, 2011.

Kankanhalli, Atreyi, Bernard C. Y. Tan, and Kwok-Kee Wei. "Contributing Knowledge to Electronic Knowledge Repositories: An Empirical Investigation." *MIS Quarterly* (2005): 113–143.

Kim, Gene, Patrick Debois, John Willis, and Jez Humble. *The DevOps Handbook: How to Create World-Class Agility, Reliability, and Security in Technology Organizations*. Portland, OR: IT Revolution, 2016.

King, John, and Roger Magoulas. *2016 Data Science Salary Survey: Tools, Trends, What Pays (and What Doesn't) for Data Professionals*. Sebastopol, CA: O'Reilly Media, 2016.

Klavens, Elinor, Robert Stroud, Eveline Oehrlich, Glenn O'Donnell, Amanda LeClair, Aaron Kinch, and Diane Kinch. *A Dangerous Disconnect: Executives Overestimate DevOps Maturity*. Cambridge, MA: Forrester, 2017.

Leek, Jeffrey. "Six Types of Analyses Every Data Scientist Should Know." *Data Scientist Insights*. January 29, 2013. https://datascientistinsights.com/2013/01/29/six-types-of-analyses-every-data-scientist-should-know/.

Leiter, Michael P., and Christina Maslach. "Early Predictors of Job Burnout and Engagement." *Journal of Applied Psychology* 93, no. 3 (2008): 498–512.

Leslie, Sarah-Jane, Andrei Cimpian, Meredith Meyer, and Edward Freeland. "Expectations of Brilliance Underlie Gender Distributions across Academic Disciplines." *Science* 347, no. 6219 (2015): 262–265.

Lindell, M. K., and D. J. Whitney. "Accounting for Common Method Variance in Cross-Sectional Research Designs." *Journal of Applied Psychology* 86, no. 1 (2001): 114–121.

Maslach, Christina. "'Understanidng Burnout,' Prof Christina Maslach (U.C. Berkely)." YouTube video. 1:12:29. Posted by Thriving in Science, December 11, 2014. https://www.youtube.com/watch?v=4kLPyV8lBbs.

McAfee, A., and E. Brynjolfsson. "Investing in the IT That Makes a Competitive Difference." *Harvard Business Review* 86, no. 7/8 (2008): 98.

McGregor, Jena. "More Women at the Top, Higher Returns." *Washington Post*. September 24, 2014. https://www.washingtonpost.com/news/on-leadership/wp/2014/09/24/more-women-at-the-top-higher-returns/?utm_term=.23c966c5241d.

Mundy, Liza. "Why Is Silicon Valley so Awful to Women?" *The Atlantic*. April 2017. https://www.theatlantic.com/magazine/archive/2017/04/why-is-silicon-valley-so-awful-to-women/517788/.

Nunnally, J. C. *Psychometric Theory*. New York: McGraw-Hill, 1978.

Panetta, Kasey. "Gartner CEO Survey." Gartner.com. April 27, 2017. https://www.gartner.com/smarterwithgartner/2017-ceo-survey-infographic/.

Perrow, Charles. *Normal Accidents: Living with High-Risk Technologies*. Princeton, NJ: Princeton University Press, 2011.

Pettigrew, A. M. "On Studying Organizational Cultures." *Administrative Science Quarterly* 24, no. 4 (1979): 570–581.

Podsakoff, P. M., and D. R. Dalton. "Research Methodology in Organizational Studies." *Journal of Management* 13, no. 2 (1987): 419–441.

Quora. "Why Women Leave the Tech Industry at a 45% Higher Rate Than Men." *Forbes*. February 28, 2017. https://www.forbes.com/sites/quora/2017/02/28/why-women-leave-the-tech-industry-at-a-45-higher-rate-than-men/#5cb8c80e4216.

Rafferty, Alannah E., and Mark A. Griffin. "Dimensions of Transformational Leadership: Conceptual and Empirical Extensions." *The Leadership Quarterly* 15, no. 3 (2004): 329–354.

Reichheld, Frederick F. "The One Number You Need to Grow." *Harvard Business Review* 81, no. 12 (2003): 46–55.

Reinertsen, Donald G. *Principles of Product Development Flow*. Redondo Beach: Celeritas Publishing, 2009.

Ries, Eric. *The Lean Startup: How Today's Entrepreneurs Use Continuous Innovation to Create Radically Successful Businesses*. New York: Crown Business, 2011.

Rock, David, and Heidi Grant. "Why Diverse Teams Are Smarter." *Harvard Business Review*. November 4, 2016. https://hbr.org/2016/11/why-diverse-teams-are-smarter.

SAGE. "SAGE Annual Salary Survey for 2007." USENIX. August 13, 2008. https://www.usenix.org/system/files/lisa/surveys/sal2007_0.pdf.

SAGE. "SAGE Annual Salary Survey for 2011." USENIX. 2012. https://www.usenix.org/system/files/lisa/surveys/lisa_2011_salary_survey.pdf.

Schwartz, Mark. *The Art of Business Value*. Portland, OR: IT Revolution Press, 2016.

Schein, E. H. *Organizational Culture and Leadership*. San Francisco: Jossey-Bass, 1985.

Shook, John. "How to Change a Culture: Lessons from NUMMI." *MIT Sloan Management Review* 51, no. 2 (2010): 63.

Smith, J. G., and J. B. Lindsay. *Beyond Inclusion: Worklife Interconnectedness, Energy, and Resilience in Organizations*. New York: Palgrave, 2014.

Snyder, Kieran. "Why Women Leave Tech: It's the Culture, Not Because 'Math Is Hard.'" *Fortune*. October 2, 2014. http://fortune.com/2014/10/02/women-leave-tech-culture/.

Stone, A. Gregory, Robert F. Russell, and Kathleen Patterson. "Transformational versus Servant Leadership: A Difference in Leader Focus." *Leadership & Organization Development Journal* 25, no. 4 (2004): 349–361.

Straub, D., M.-C. Boudreau, and D. Gefen. "Validation Guidelines for IS Positivist Research." *Communications of the AIS* 13 (2004): 380–427.

Stroud, Rob, and Elinor Klavens with Eveline Oehrlich, Aaron Kinch, and Diane Lynch. *DevOps Heat Map 2017*. Cambridge, MA: Forrester, 2017. https://www.forrester.com/report/DevOps+Heat+Map+2017/-/E-RES137782.

This American Life, episode 561. "NUMMI 2015." Aired July 17, 2015. https://www.thisamericanlife.org/radio-archives/episode/561/nummi-2015.

Ulrich, D., and B. McKelvey. "General Organizational Classification: An Empirical Test Using the United States and Japanese Electronic Industry." *Organization Science* 1, no. 1 (1990): 99–118.

Ward, J. H. "Hierarchical Grouping to Optimize an Objective Function." *Journal of the American Statistical Association* 58 (1963): 236–244.

Wardley, Simon. "An Introduction to Wardley (Value Chain) Mapping." *Bits or Pieces?* blog. February 2, 2015. http://blog.gardeviance.org/2015/02/an-introduction-to-wardley-value-chain.html.

Weinberg, Gerald M. *Quality Software Management. Volume 1: Systems Thinking*. New York: Dorset House Publishing, 1992.

Westrum, Ron. "A Typology of Organisational Cultures." *Quality and Safety in Health Care* 13, no. suppl 2 (2004): ii22–ii27.

Westrum, Ron. "The Study of Information Flow: A Personal Journey." *Safety Science* 67 (2014): 58–63.

Wickett, James. "Attacking Pipelines—Security Meets Continuous Delivery." Slideshare.net, June 11, 2014. http://www.slideshare.net/wickett/attacking-pipelinessecurity-meets-continuous-delivery.

Widener, Sally K. "An Empirical Analysis of the Levers of Control Framework." *Accounting, Organizations and Society* 32, no. 7 (2007): 757–788.

Woolley, Anita, and T. Malone. "Defend Your Research: What Makes a Team Smarter? More Women." *Harvard Business Review* (June 2011).

Yegge, Steve. "Stevey's Google Platform Rant." GitHub gist. 2011. https://gist.github.com/jezhumble/a8b3cbb4ea20139582fa8ffc9d791fb2.

INDEX

D

E

F

G

H

I

J

K

L

M

P

Q

R

S

T

U

V

W

Y

ABOUT THE AUTHORS

Dr. Nicole Forsgren is CEO and Chief Scientist at DevOps Research and Assessment. She is best known as the lead investigator on the largest DevOps studies to date. She has been a professor and performance engineer and her work has been published in several peer-reviewed journals.

Jez Humble is coauthor of *The DevOps Handbook*, *Lean Enterprise*, and the Jolt Award-winning *Continuous Delivery*. He is currently researching how to build high-performing teams at his startup, DevOps Research and Assessment, LLC, and teaching at UC Berkeley.

Gene Kim is a multiple award-winning CTO, researcher, and author of *The Phoenix Project*, *The DevOps Handbook*, and *The Visible Ops Handbook*. He is founder of IT Revolution and is the founder and host of the DevOps Enterprise Summit conferences.